BAD COMPANY

The strange cult of the CEO

Gideon Haigh is the author of two other books on
business: *The Battle for BHP* and *One of a Kind: The Story of Bankers
Trust Australia*. He is also a renowned writer on cricket,
whose book *Mystery Spinner*, his acclaimed biography of the
maverick spin bowler Jack Iverson (also published by
Aurum, along with *The Big Ship*, a biography of the
legendary Australian Test captain Warwick Armstrong, and
Many a Slip: The Diary of a Club Cricket Season), was voted the
Cricket Society's Book of the Year and described as
'a classic' by the *Sunday Times*. He has written for
The Times and the *Financial Times* and contributes
regularly to the *Guardian*.

BAD COMPANY

The strange cult of the CEO

GIDEON HAIGH

$$$

First published in Great Britain
2004 by Aurum Press Ltd
25 Bedford Avenue, London WC1B 3AT

An earlier version of this work was published in *Quarterly Essay* 10
in Australia by Black Inc.

A catalogue record for this book is available from the British Library.

ISBN 1 85410 949 9

1 3 5 7 9 10 8 6 4 2
2004 2006 2008 2007 2005

Designed in Joanna 11 on 13pt by Geoff Green Book Design
Printed in Great Britain by Bookmarque, Croydon, Surrey

Contents

$$$

Prologue

'*A*re you smart?'
'I am fucking smart.'
'Are you ambitious?'
'I am fucking ambitious.'

Among the many stories concerning him, the one about his exchange with an admissions officer from Harvard University seemed to contain all anybody needed to know about Jeffrey Skilling. At the time, Skilling had been a young banker in quest of the Harvard MBA that would equip him at the tony management consultants, McKinseys. By the time the catechism entered corporate lore, Skilling had surrounded himself with intelligence, ambition and profane cockiness at Enron, the Houston energy-trading dynamo that preened itself as the 'World's Leading Company'. Congregating Enronites would listen dutifully to their folksy figurehead Ken Lay, but it was the gospel according to CEO Skilling, as much evangelist as entrepreneur, that they came to hear:

> He was dressed casually, almost carelessly, like his troops, and he wore his hair combed off his face in the style of Hollywood producers and Wall Street financiers. He was assiduously fit; his eyes were ice blue and his gaze was

I

steady, and he spoke in clipped, flat, supremely confident tones. Everyone at Enron knew that Jeff was twice as smart as they were – twice as smart as they could ever hope to be – and they hung on every word.

It was Skilling who had made the revenues grow from $4 billion to more than $60 billion, an increase of nearly 2000 per cent. It was Skilling who had made the stock price ascend to the heavens. So it was Skilling who made Enron's troops frantic to live in fast-forward mode, who made them anxious to prove that they could deliver any concept he could dream up.... Because if Jeff Skilling thought you 'got it', you really did.

If you 'got' Jeff Skilling, meanwhile, you were similarly endowed. 'Power Broker' was the headline on *Businessweek's* cover when Skilling appeared, in hipper-than-thou black from head to toe, electricity coursing through his body. *Worth* judged the 'hypersmart' and 'hyperconfident' Skilling to be second only to Microsoft's Steve Ballmer among American CEOs; when he bounded on stage at a big technology conference in Las Vegas in June 2001 he was heralded as 'the number one CEO in the country'. Nor could the business press be accused of undue credulity; their celebrations amplified only slightly the claims of others far closer to the action. Enron embodied a new business model – fast, edgy, virtual, vital – that had overthrown the old order, symbolised in its plush London offices at Grosvenor Gardens, home during the day of dark satanic nationalised industries to the National Coal Board. Investors looked on with benign indifference, even admiration, as Enron's executives became millionaires many times over: Skilling himself collected $190 million in three years in sales of Enron stock. Management consultants, an industry erected on a similar *amour propre*, rushed to endorse Skilling's belief in the premium that talent deserved: 'We hire very smart people and we pay them more than they think they are worth.' Within Enron there pertained what one executive called 'the Kleig-Light syndrome': 'Wherever Jeff was, talent would flock. The activity was following the light.' In one moment of heady narcissism, Skilling himself was heard to exult: 'I am Enron!'

This close personal identification with Enron had many entailments. Skilling lived and died by Enron's profile on Wall Street. He anguished over its quarterly earnings statements. He experienced fluctuations in its share price as personal reflections:

> When it rose, he was exultant; when it dropped, he was glum. Whenever he was on the road, Skilling would call several times a day just to check on how the stock was performing.... As a businessman his thought process revolved almost entirely around the stock, to the point where he began to believe that Enron's market capitalisation... was the only measure the company should be concerned with.

In some respects, mostly the wrong ones, Skilling's idée fixe was quite sensible. Enron had been rated by *Fortune* as 'America's most innovative corporation' for five consecutive years. But its deepest well of innovation was the one from which its accounts were drawn. Enron's balance sheet resembled one of those eerily perfected Hollywood bodies: assets toned, chiselled, and always shot from the right angles; liabilities tastefully liposuctioned away. And, because of its successful campaign to adopt mark-to-market accounting, everything was undergirded by share price, from the security on its debt to the extraordinary rewards it showered on the favoured – not to mention Skilling's perception of himself.

It was the last that came under pressure first when Enron's value began declining during a general market subsidence in 2001. Skilling became taciturn, erratic. He began lamenting his job's personal toll. He would plead with departing colleagues to stay, and weep while complaining of internal rivals too powerful for him to control. He drank and smoked heavily, and arrived at work one day so dishevelled and despairing that Lay sent him home. When he finally resigned, it was so eagerly that he left a $20 million severance package on the table.

Part of the rest of this story is history. Like Lady Brett Ashley's fiancé Michael in Hemingway's *The Sun Also Rises*, Enron went broke 'gradually and then suddenly'. Skilling's decision sent the first tremor through employees and investors that could not be ignored: it was in response to his departure that Enron's Cassandra, Sherron Watkins, composed the first of her famous memoranda to Lay. Doubt and debt metastasised: restated earnings, reconsolidated borrowings, downgraded creditworthiness, diminished counterparty status. By November 2001, what had been America's seventh-biggest company had become America's biggest bankruptcy. Four thousand employees lost their jobs; within months, 85,000 at Enron's accomplice, accounting firm Arthur Andersen, had lost theirs as well.

The other part of the story is necessarily more conjectural. Since it became a byword for corporate sleaze, Enron has been investigated by the Justice Department, the Securities and Exchange Commission, the Department of Labor, the Federal Energy Regulatory Commission, and the state of California. Politicians, lawyers, Wall Street regulators, bankruptcy examiners and investigative journalists have sifted its debris trying to work out what went wrong, moving mountains in the process: Enron's last tax return, for example, ran to thirteen volumes. Skilling, naturally, has been the object of many of these inquiries, and in the foreground of many of the pictures painted – yet, confoundingly, he has been as conspicuous in his absence as in his presence. Lines of authority and communication have resisted reconstruction. Incriminating documentation has proven elusive. In a company that purported to be ahead of technological evolution, Skilling seems to have been a veritable troglodyte. He never surfed the net. He declined to use email. He only used the two computer screens on his desk to track stock and commodity prices ('He didn't even know how to turn them on,' said his secretary). It's far from clear of what deals Skilling was a champion, partly because he applied his signature sparingly, partly because his temperament was so mercurial. In the words of one recent account: 'He sometimes praised deals that had been carried out against his orders. He became enraptured with businesses he had initially dismissed. And he sometimes insisted he'd always opposed deals he'd actually embraced.' When conference discussions dwelt on detail, it is said, Skilling's eyes would glaze over. 'Just do it!' he would erupt when he felt he'd ignored enough. 'Just get it done!' On one occasion he met with executives from Enron Energy Services and told them that their business would be worth $500 million in the next few years. Asked how, he retorted: 'You guys are the creative ones. That's what you guys have to figure out.' His judgement was scrutinised so seldom not because of his depth of knowledge when questioned but because of his severity of response when challenged. 'He had a good McKinsey trick,' an analyst has recalled. 'If you asked a question he didn't want to answer he would dump a ton of data on you. But he didn't answer. If you were brave and still said you didn't get it, he would turn on you. "Well, it's so obvious," he would say. "How can you not get it?" ' Sceptics were dismissed as jeremiahs in tirades like one taped by Bethany MacLean, the young *Fortune* writer who first had the nerve to ask 'Is Enron Overpriced?': 'We are doing it purely right… people who raise questions are people who have not gone through our business in detail… people who don't understand want to throw rocks at us.... Anyone who is successful, people would like to take them down based on ignorance.'

The irony is that ignorance has now become Skilling's defence. At first the vaporising of a $100 billion company had all the hallmarks of the crime of the century. The trail was said to lead all the way to the White House – this being Texas, probably via the grassy knoll. But while some lower-ranked treasury executives are behind bars and chief financial officer Andrew Fastow, a millionaire Milo Minderbinder, has been indicted, no action has been taken against Enron's leaders. Skilling, it is true, sold $67 million in Enron stock while the going was good. But he did so legally and visibly under an SEC-supervised program, then stopped in June 2001, apparently convinced that the stock was undervalued: a conviction that cost him almost as much as he made. And while Enron seemed in the tradition of financial suicides like Barings and Sumitomo, it was not obviously the victim of the classic 'rogue trader'; this was, instead, a 'rogue organisation'. As Atlanta attorney Neil Batson has concluded in his role as bankruptcy examiner: 'The transactions at issue were complex and massive, and large groups of officers and employees, representing such diverse functions as finance, accounting, tax and legal, were assembled to complete them.' Among the evidence his report reproduces are the lyrics of a song, 'Balance Sheet Blues', which circulated within Enron during 1998: 'They call us 'innovators'/We got to please the raters/Don't feed us to the 'gators/We got the Balance Sheet Blues.' Batson notes: 'While plainly satirical, this song reflects an appreciation of key factors that ultimately contributed to Enron's demise: excessive leverage, a voracious appetite for cash and reliance on inadequately disclosed financial transactions.'

Media coverage of the investigation now exudes a growing frustration. The collapse of a company is one thing; the failure to perp walk and punish a villain quite another.

'Somebody needs to go to jail,' hectored senate majority leader Tom Daschle after Enron's collapse; the meagre dividends of prosecutions since have become a kind of reproach for all who run and regulate public companies. 'In the end,' reported Jeffrey Toobin in the *New Yorker* recently, 'prosecutors may be able to show only that Lay and Skilling presided over a culture where this kind of pervasive dishonesty flourished – which is not, in any legal sense, a crime.' To a disconcerting degree, it would seem, behaviours at Enron were exceptional only in their extremity, rather than in their nature. Everyone at the time was manipulating their accounts, striving to hit quarterly earnings targets, pumping their share prices, paying themselves exorbitantly. As the economic historian Peter Temin has characterised it: 'Enron didn't get caught. Enron was so far out on the edge it fell off.'

Amid it all, the fate of Jeffrey Skilling, perhaps the most despised CEO of his generation, keeps everyone wondering. He was the man who personified Enron like no other. He was the mastermind who held the employees, investors and observers alike in his spell. Yet much of his magniloquence and effrontery has been revealed since as a pretence, a performance, a creation of others. Skilling may still be arraigned and brought to book. In some ways he has already been sentenced, by a posterity that distinguishes, not without good reason, between legal and moral obligations. This leaves unexplored, however, the dimension of practical accountability. What might it mean that it has proven so hard to establish cause and effect and to distribute blame and shame in a case as egregious as Enron? If business failure is so complex, what might be inferred about business success? If it sounds like a form of exculpation to propose that CEOs aren't as bad as we are inclined to imagine them, does it also follow that they were not, are not and never will be as good as they, others and, it should be admitted, we ourselves have pretended?

Fat Cats

$$$

In these days of rage with the CEO, it is worth recalling that disillusionment cannot arise without prior faith. Not so long ago, when we were still toasting the *belle époque* in equities, many figures now reviled were revered – often by those who should have known better. When WorldCom's market value peaked, President Bill Clinton accepted an invitation to its headquarters from founder Bernie Ebbers. 'I came here today because you are the symbol of 21st century America,' Clinton eulogised. 'You are the embodiment of what I want for the future.' Philosophies that would scarcely dare express themselves today were playing to packed houses, even in Britain. 'We need to recognise,' Trade and Industry Secretary Stephen Byers told a City audience in July 1999, 'that in a global economy, world-class performance must be rewarded with world-class pay.... We accept such an approach in relation to sports stars: so why don't we adopt the same attitude for directors? To attract world-class players, we need to pay at world-class levels.'

Some aspects of this celebration have survived. If we are not in thrall to business, we are certainly complicit in its model of the world. Business rhetoric pervades the language of our politicians, our professionals, our academics, even our athletes. Business customs have infiltrated schools, universities, the public service, even volunteer organisations. Business schools churn out newly minted MBAs. Bookshops where the history of the world is crammed into a shelf devote whole walls to books with titles like *How To Become CEO*, *How to Act Like a CEO*, and *CEO Logic: How to Think and Act Like a Chief Executive*. Business leadership, publishers would have us believe, is a timeless art, practised since antiquity, even if its exponents – such as Jesus Christ, Sun Tzu, Alexander the Great, Sir Ernest Shackleton, General George Patton, Thomas Jefferson and Elizabeth I – were unaware of their acumen.

We have, furthermore, seldom been more infatuated with the principles and practice of leadership, often the first craving of uncertain times – and its corporate model is one we are accustomed to saluting. Businessmen, we feel, for all those behaviours that make us uneasy and squeamish, do seem to get things done. Got a problem? Call for a CEO. Tax system in strife? Get that chap Martin Taylor from Barclays. Tory party in disarray? Grab Archie Norman from Asda. English cricket a national embarrassment? Call in Tesco's Lord McLaurin. Even now, indeed, there remains an aspect of CEOs we find strangely appealing: we know what they stand for. They are not trying to win popularity contests – or, at least, not so unctuously as our elected representatives. They merely want our money. In a world of ambiguities and paradoxes, there is something to be said for nakedness – even if it be merely nakedness of greed.

This explains, at least partly, why corporate leadership as preparation for high office, like military leadership before it, seems an idea whose time has come, even in a period of unease about commercial mores. Some have succeeded in the transition, like Silvio Berlusconi swapping Fininvest for Forza Italia; some have failed, like Hyundai founder Chung Ju Yung in South Korea; some have blossomed into statesmen: United Nations secretary-general Kofi Annan has a master's in management from MIT, and once ran the Ghana Tourist Development Company. And they do give us a curious confidence; thus the contemporary trend to political leaders looking more like CEOs. Serbian prime minister Zoran Djindjic was known to his countrymen as 'the Manager'. Even Her Majesty, it is said, refers privately to the House of Windsor as 'the Family Firm'.

The nexus is especially strong in the US, where the phrase 'chief executive' originated about 150 years ago to denote the president himself. Vice-president Dick Cheney (energy services group Halliburton), commerce secretary Don Evans (energy services group Tom Brown), labor secretary Elaine Chan (United Way of America), White House chief-of-staff Andrew Card (American Automobile Manufacturers Association), treasury secretary John Snow (CSX) and defence secretary Donald Rumsfeld (General Instruments and pharmaceutical group G. D. Searle) are all *quondam* CEOs. Rumsfeld actually featured in *Fortune*'s original intake of 'America's Ten Toughest Bosses' in April 1980; *The Rumsfeld Way* (2001) suggests that he persecutes corporate bureaucracies as vehemently as any 'axis of evil'. Though at the height of hostilities in Iraq there were many dark mutterings about the malign influence of religion in the White House, the Bush administration is more a CEOcracy than theocracy – before Bush, no American president since Eisenhower had more than one CEO in the cabinet, and Eisenhower only had two. Bush himself, of course, is not only the first president to hold a Harvard MBA, but the first to have been investigated by the Securities and Exchange Commission. Whatever the US's hegemonic pretensions in the Middle East, its leaders are restrained by fiscal rectitude. These days, even war has to come in on time and on budget.

In a society where we look one another right in the wallet, CEOs certainly stand tall: seldom in history can a caste have been rewarded so richly. When Graef Crystal published a wide-ranging critique of executive remuneration in 1991, describing a twenty-year period in which American CEOs had hiked their own pay 400 per cent, he called it *In Search of Excess*. No one had to search far: CEO compensation in the US surged another 535 per cent in the 1990s. In part, this was a natural outcome of the increasing use of equity in the form of stock options as a component of remuneration during a period of strong share-price appreciation. But only in part – the increase actually outstripped all conceivable correlatives. The value of the top five hundred stocks increased about 300 per cent over the same period, while profits about doubled, and average weekly wages grew only a third. When Crystal published his critique, the standard big company CEO in the US earned 140 times the pay of the average worker; the multiple is now nearer 500 times. Strenuous efforts have been made to give compensation the appearance of the subtlest science. Committees are constituted, consultants retained, and pay has increased in variety as well as quantum. But the results always seem burnished by the common shade of gold: golden hellos, golden goodbyes, golden handcuffs, golden handshakes, and, most controversially, golden parachutes, a severance package to which one usually becomes entitled on change of control, or should matters go awry. According to a *USA Today* survey, the average compensation package for CEOs in the top 100 American companies in 2002 was $33.4 million – nearly a third banked more than $50 million in salaries, bonuses and shares. The Corporate Library, a shareholders' ginger group, estimates that the average departing CEO in 2002 was gifted a $16.5 million severance package.

Britain has always tended to look askance at American corporate mores – sometimes with envy, sometimes with a smidgeon of scorn. Figures for growth rates in British executive pay suggest that the former is in the ascendant. In the last decade the average earnings of CEOs at FTSE-100 companies have increased almost 300 per cent, while wages among British employees as a whole have grown about 45 per cent. The pace of increase, moreover, seems to be picking up, without regard to the fortunes of shareholders. A *Guardian* survey of executive pay in 2003 revealed a symmetry almost too exquisite, executive pay having grown twenty-three per cent in 2002 as share prices fell twenty-four per cent. Crude calculation reveals some striking relativities: *The Observer* estimated recently that the chairman of Rentokil, Sir Clive Thompson, was paid the equivalent of 247 of his employees.

The beneficiaries of these pay trends, at least, have encountered no difficulty in rationalising them. A recent poll of *Fortune* 1000 CEOs revealed that 87 per cent thought their pay condign; eleven per cent thought they were still underpaid, and only two per cent confessed to feeling over-rewarded. For criticism, they have shown open disdain. Eight top American CEOs were invited in May 2003 to appear before a Senate hearing exploring the issue of executive pay: not one showed up. Jean-Pierre Garnier, the CEO of GlaxoSmithKline, disposed of detractors with Gallic insouciance: 'If you pay peanuts you get monkeys. And we cannot have monkeys running this company.'

It is an indication of the temper of the times, however, that such standard defences are raising, not defusing, ire. Big business is accustomed to being last to get credit for people feeling good, and first to suffer blame when people feel bad – but seldom can it have endured rage of such incandescence. In her *j'accuse*, *Pigs at the Trough* (2003), Arianna Huffington envisions a suburb, CEOville, whose residents have subtly revised the Declaration of Independence to read: 'All men are endowed by their creator with certain inalienable rights, that among these are stock options, golden parachutes, and the reckless pursuit of limitless wealth.' Bill Flanagan begins his tirade, *Dirty Rotten CEOs* (2003), with a tour of a imaginary torture chamber cum theme park, Greed World, where notorious bosses are broken on wheels and boiled in black oil: 'There are surely millions of folks who would love to see those dirty, rotten CEOs suffer punishments only a medieval Pope could dream up.' In a recent series on 'family-friendly' Pax TV, *Just Cause*, an avenging paralegal was entrusted with 'cleaning up America... one crooked CEO at a time' – at that rate, it could run and run.

While public anger can usually be forborne, investor anger is generally less tractable – and so it is proving. Warren Buffett, the Berkshire Hathaway billionaire, has called the issue of executive compensation 'the acid test of reform', and enjoined shareholders to 'rise up' against greedy chief executives; they seem to have heeded him. Time was when nothing short of fire or flood could upend an American CEO. Yet the US has recently been treated to a phenomenon almost without precedent: top executives defenestrated by restive shareholders and boards simply because of the scale of their booty. May 2003 brought the hurried resignation of Jeffrey Barbakow, CEO at Californian hospital managers Tenet Healthcare, who while his company's stock had depreciated 60 per cent was availing himself of $111 million through exercising stock options. June spelled the end for Don Carty, CEO of American Airlines, who had celebrated wringing $1.8 billion in pay cuts and job losses from the company's workers by scattering lucrative retention bonuses among his executive cabal – a gesture too crass even in corporate America. That Richard Grasso was chairman of the New York Stock Exchange gave his fall an added piquancy: capitalism had been bearded in its own den. Grasso, who stood to receive $140 million in accumulated benefits, belatedly sought redemption by forgoing another

$48 million due to him. It was too little too late after so much so soon.

The Buffett challenge has also been taken up with surprising ardour in Britain, where shareholders have been less strident but just as uniformly critical: four in five respondents to a recent poll thought CEOs were overpaid. Investors were unusually truculent during the 2003 annual meeting season, taking advantage for the first time of legislation allowing them to vent views on remuneration packages. According to Pirc, the corporate advisory group, more than twenty companies endured protest votes in excess of 20 per cent against their remuneration reports last year, which, given the reputation of shareholders for supine behaviour, amounts almost to blood in the streets. Garnier, the Glaxo organ-grinder, became the most public target of dissidence. A majority of investors condemned a package he had sought worth £22 million in the event of premature dismissal; he was compelled to accept a revised and reduced package just before Christmas. Directors at Royal Sun Alliance and Tesco were also made to squirm. Particular asperity in public and press comment was reserved for what Patricia Hewitt, Secretary of State for Trade and Industry, called 'rewards for failure': big pay-offs proposed for departing CEOs preparatory to big lay-offs among employees, like those handed to Telewest's Adam Singer, Granada's Steve Morrison and Cable & Wireless's Graham Wallace. At least one CEO, Paul Anderson of BHP Billiton, was moved to describe executive remuneration as 'totally out of control' – just, mind you, as he was about to pocket a £3.54 million gratuity for services rendered.

In some respects, it should be seen, these are the recent eruptions in a story that has bubbled away on business pages for a decade and more. As CEOs have hiked their own pay, so the market has hiked its expectations, motivating CEOs as

Voltaire once said the British urged its admirals on: with occasional executions *pour encourager les autres*. In his *Capitalism Against Capitalism* (1993), Michel Albert observed: 'They [CEOs] have become personalities in a drama, and they must live up to the script or disappoint an audience of millions.' The script has only grown lengthier, the audience more critical, and disappointment more contagious. In a comprehensive worldwide survey last year, management consultants Booz Allen Hamilton found that 'involuntary, performance-related' turnover in 2002 accounted for two in every five CEO successions – a 70 per cent increase on the previous year. 'Forced CEO succession,' the authors concluded, 'has become "the new normal".' According to corporate-relations group Burson-Marsteller, CEOs entrusted with turnarounds will in most instances have only one chance to make a mark: the market allows about eight months to develop a strategy, nineteen months to bolster the share price, twenty-one months to improve earnings. If nothing has changed, or not enough, the process is repeated. This phenomenon, which the organisational theorists Warren Bennis and James O'Toole have christened 'CEO churning', has some powerful proponents. Warren Buffett led the putsch to oust Doug Ivester in December 1999 after eighteen wretched months at Coca-Cola; leveraged buy-out king Henry Kravis instigated the exit of Michael Hawley in October 2000, after a similar spell at Gillette; it was William Clay Ford Jnr, no less, who in October 2001 seized the controls at the corporation founded by his great-grandfather when its boss of less than three years, Jac Nasser, threatened to run it off the road. A disaffected market demands its due, sometimes not so much for current underperformance, as past over-optimism. Three years after the show-stopping $106 billion amalgamation of AOL with Time Warner, its architects Steve Case, Gerald Levin and Bob Pittman paid with their jobs for presiding over history's biggest loss, $98.7 billion. No new strategic direction was promised; their departures were more in the nature of propitiation.

The dissolution of the dotcoms in April 2000, followed by the collapse in the value of telco assets, was always likely to end a few careers: the collusion of docile auditors, credulous analysts and supine shareholders made it inevitable. Ultimately more disturbing, perhaps, has been the abiding addiction to management change developed by business names of apparent permanence and rectitude. When Kmart's founder Sebastian S. Kresge incorporated his chain of dime stores in 1916, he publicly espoused principles he claimed to have gleaned from his bee hives: 'My bees always remind me that hard work, thrift, sobriety, and an earnest struggle to live an upright Christian life are the first rungs on the ladder of success.' He would wear pairs of shoes until they literally fell apart, gave up golf because he could not stand to lose the balls, and went to his reward in his hundredth year, by which time his empire extended to almost a thousand stores. How that ethos had changed by the time Kmart sought a new chief in 1980 to restore momentum to stalled sales growth. A succession of CEOs came and went, paid ever more, and achieving ever less. The last, Chuck Conaway, went on what one account described as 'a two-year program of deceit, intimidation and unauthorised spending'; more than $12 million, for example, was spent on corporate airplanes. Worse still, chairman Conaway and his president Mark Schwartz lavished $850 million on new merchandise for an ill-conceived price war with Wal-Mart – the company filed for Chapter 11 in January 2002 after announcing a $2.42 billion loss.

At one time, Europeans would have deplored the wastage inherent in *le capitalisme sauvage du modele anglo-saxon*. Yet attrition in their CEO ranks has recently been almost as great. In

France, entertainment mogul manqué Jean-Marie Messier was sacked from Vivendi Universal for his thriftless ways. In Germany, Thomas Middelhoff lost his job at Bertelsmann after estranging its powerful Mohn family. France Telecom, Deutsche Telekom and Telecom Italia all churned bosses within eighteen months. Former market favourites like Switzerland's BZ Group, Sweden's ABB, the Netherlands' Royal Ahold, Italy's Parmalat and Russia's Yukos have all, for various reasons, had to drop the pilot. Corporate comeuppance has even become a feature of Asian business, with the ousting of Tokyo Electric Power's Nobuya Minami, China State Power's Gao Yan, and the indictments for accounting fraud at SK Group, South Korea's third-largest *chaebol*. In Canada, Hollinger's Lord Black, proprietor of Telegraph Newspapers, came off the worse in a wrangle with investment group Tweedy Browne over his flair for generosity to himself. And in Australia, ritual executive sacrifice has caught on with a vengeance: the average CEO now lasts about four years. A quarter of Australia's top 100 companies have turned over their bosses in the last two years. Leighton Constructions' Wal King has likened meetings of the bosses' talking shop, the Business Council of Australia, to Alzheimer's Disease: you're always making new friends.

Anger about pay is an outcome of more recent stresses. It is about unequal distribution – of money, and of pain, given that bosses seem to have been left largely untouched by the sufferings of shareholders. In general, shareholders have been incredibly tolerant of surging CEO rewards. In one famous incident at the height of the boom, Roberto Goizueta stood up at the annual meeting of Coca-Cola and was interrupted four times while explaining his $80 million pay packet – by applause. Nobody looked twice at pay's northwards heading until it continued after the stockmarket itself headed south. The mix of regulation and retribution that followed the first wave of scandals, at Enron, WorldCom, Adelphia, Tyco and telcos too numerous to name, was concerned chiefly with the integrity of financial statements and the independence of auditors: the Sarbanes-Oxley Act rushed into law by US Congress in July 2002, requiring that CEOs and CFOs swear in front of a notary that their latest annual and quarterly filings contain no 'untrue statement' and omit no 'material fact', did not directly touch on compensation, and has in any event so far produced only one indictment: HealthSouth's Richard Scrushy. Pay is not, however, an entirely inappropriate focus for a critique of CEOs. Malpractice sustains our interest only so long, and can be countered by the 'few bad apples' theory, which however unconvincing is always a comfort (thus Patricia Hewitt's view: 'Britain has some of the best and most successful business in the world. But the reputation of the majority is being tarnished by the minority'). Pay cannot be so lightly ignored. Every CEO is paid *a lot*; pay is eternal; pay is a conducting rod for criticism.

Merely to be angry about pay, however, is insufficient. The problem with anger is that it loses spirit, loses focus and subsides. Sound and fury will end up signifying nothing; recrimination will not relieve discontents or mend flawed models of corporate governance. This short book attempts instead to explain, as simply and coolly as possible, why we have the CEOs we do and why we pay them so much. It is for this reason, and reasons like it, that it will be oriented toward the United States, not necessarily because of that country's claims to political or cultural leadership, but because it is, as Dean Rusk put it, 'the fat boy in the canoe': when it moves, all must adjust. To speak of CEOs at all, it is worth noting, is to enfold an American idea of corporate command. The expression actually took less time to sweep the world than it did the US. The title CEO did not achieve widespread use in American companies until the 1970s, when it began to be attached to the more traditional titles of chairman and president. But once it became common coin in the US, established variants in the rest of the world, such as secretary, general manager and managing director, fell steadily into desuetude; Canadian organisational theorist Henry Mintzberg has commented drily that what we often call globalisation is more often simply 'American management spreading round the globe'.

One might speculate, *en passant*, how business nomenclature contributes to practice and perception. As the Edwardian investor Sir Ernest Cassel once pointed out, it often does: 'When I was young people called me a gambler. As the scale of my operations increased, I became known as a speculator. Now I am called a banker. But I have been doing the same thing all the time.' The different names allocated to our captains of industry similarly suggest a progression of sorts. 'Secretary' sounded like a flunkey, 'general manager' like a factotum, and even 'managing director' was no better than *primus inter pares*. The self-reinforcing trinity of 'chief executive officer' is invested with majesty by near-tautology, the chief, the executive and the officer all exuding independent senses of seniority and authority. Especially when the title is shortened and sharpened to CEO, it suggests a figure born to lead, just as a chairman sounds designed to sit. And lead they do, just as we fall in step behind them.

Rich White Men

$$\$\$\$$

Who are CEOs, and from where do they come? At the simplest level, big businesses are still run overwhelmingly by men. Women who've bubbled to the surface, such as Anita Roddick, Ann Iverson, Carly Fiorina, Marjorie Scardino and Margaret Whitman, have tended to attract more attention than their companies – to their advantage in good times, to their detriment in bad. *The Economist* has described them as facing a vicious circle: 'There are not enough female executives, which means that those who do emerge, get over-hyped, which increases the chance of failure (real or perceived), which makes companies more nervous about appointing female chief executives.' This partly explains why female CEOs have seldom differentiated themselves significantly from the male of the species, even in terms of susceptibility to the temptations of corporate excess: witness the $50 million that Jill Barad collected after presiding over a disastrous acquisition at toy giant Mattel, and the $44 million 'golden parachute' that made Linda Wachner unsackable at fading fashion group Warnaco.

It could be said that women shape corporations in other ways. For instance, the three most admired American bosses of the last twenty years – Wal-Mart's Sam Walton, IBM's Lou Gerstner and General Electric's Jack Welch – were raised in matriduxies. Walton's mother was 'a pretty special motivator' who was 'extremely ambitious for her kids'; Gerstner's 'drove us toward excellence, accomplishment and success' by being 'enormously disciplined, hard-working, and ambitious for all her children'; Welch's fortified him with 'blunt, unyielding admonitions that ring in my head every day', and habits for which he later became renowned: 'She checked constantly to see if I did my homework, in much the same way that I continually follow up work today.' Before you rush to the conclusion that behind every great CEO stands a mighty matriarch, though, Walton, Gerstner and Welch shared this influence with perhaps the most notorious American CEO of recent times. The restlessly extrovert Al Dunlap, corporate credits stretching from Scott Paper to Sunbeam, was blessed with an 'opinionated and introverted' mother who 'doted on his every need'. 'After high school dates,' reported his biographer John Byrne, 'Dunlap would come home to sit at the foot of her bed and speak expansively about his day and his life.'

Conjectures about what makes a successful CEO have an irritating habit of collapsing in the face of the eternal exception: one is inclined to say that this generalisation is true except in all the cases where it isn't. Some have proposed that it is a recommendation to have a nourishing spiritual belief. Walton, Gerstner and Welch all came from religious households: Walton was a Methodist, Welch and Gerstner strict Catholics. Again, though, American religion is a coat of many colours. WorldCom's Bernie Ebbers and Enron's Ken Lay were also Bible-bashing Baptists: Ebbers began board and stockholder meetings with a prayer; Lay, a preacher's son, solemnly declared during the Californian power crisis: 'I believe in God and I believe in free markets.' It is simplest to admit that the backgrounds of successful business leaders present few obvious patterns. Most guides to the brains behind corporations reveal little beyond their conventionality. In *Entering Tiger Country* (2000), their survey of 'how ideas are shaped in an organisation', Jean Lammiman and Michael Syrett turned up some strikingly unenlightening information: a sixth of CEOs surveyed had found business inspiration through a fictional character, a fifth through a historical personage like Winston Churchill, while more than half had had their best ideas while in relaxed settings like travelling, walking the dog or listening to music. Which made them sound like... well, like everybody else. In *The Mind of the CEO* (2001), Jeffrey Garten sought to demonstrate that 'top business leaders are the people who best understand the effects of change, technology, globalisation'. Yet he found them even duller on the subject than most politicians, and platitudinous on everything else. It's not even as though CEOs are distinguished by superior intelligence – a puzzle that perplexed the first American executive paid more than $1 million, Charles Schwab, US Steel's inaugural president, a century ago: 'Here I am, a not over-good business man, a second-rate engineer. I can make poor mechanical drawings. I play the piano after a fashion. In fact, I am one of those proverbial jack-of-all-trades who are usually failures. Why I am not, I can't tell you.'

It is by what they do, rather than who they are, that CEOs differentiate themselves. Mark Twain once observed that if work were so great 'the rich would have hogged it long ago'. A glance at the modern CEO suggests they might have. Three-quarters of American CEOs work more than sixty hours a week. They start early. Hewlett-Packard's Fiorina rises at 4.30am and jogs on a treadmill while checking her e-mails. They finish late. DaimlerChrysler's Jurgen Schrempp believes in disarming managers with alcohol: 'You never hear the truth from your subordinates until after ten in the evening.' Stories of the work habits of some CEOs beggar belief. Mind you, as the British researchers Roy Lewis and Rosemary Stewart once noted, days that become nights are easier to bear when it is a schedule of one's own design:

> Because work is such fun to the boss, he can work long hours absorbed, happy and tireless. Few bosses realise, however, that they enjoy this pleasure at the expense of everyone else; that, lower down, to do half the boss's stint is thrice as tiring. On the contrary, it is a wonder to most business men who have wealth and sit permanently in the driver's seat that everyone else — at least among their executives — is not just as 'keen'. Bosses commonly talk of the 'shared adventure' of their enterprise. Yet it cannot really be shared — though nobody will dare to tell the boss this horrid truth.

Hearth and home are redesigned round the contours of executive duty. 'You live in a constant state of guilt,' Craig Conway of Peoplesoft has said. 'Either you are not devoting enough time to your family or you are not devoting enough time to the business.' Private lives, though, must remain so, and where they don't can be costly. Sir Ralph Halpern is remembered today for tabloid revelations of his 'five-times-a-night' assignations with a blonde model as much as for his leadership of Burton Group. The image of domestic serenity, in fact, is not merely advisable, it can work in one's favour. As Michael Eisner sought the top job at Disney, a family photo in a wholesome magazine profile was crucial; when big investor Sid Bass saw it, the image 'reassured him that I didn't fit the stereotype of a wild, partying Hollywood executive'.

As far as recreation is concerned, the traditional diversion has been golf, usually with business talked as fairways are traversed: Andrew Carnegie was persuaded to throw in his lot with J. P. Morgan's US Steel after a successful round at Manhattan's St Andrews. 'I've met some of the world's greatest human beings playing golf,' opines Jack Welch in *Straight From*

The Gut (2001), revealing that part of the selection process for his successor at General Electric was a golf day with directors – suitable candidates, by definition, played a decent game. But times are changing. Profiling a new generation of bosses recently, *Fortune* reported: 'Shockingly, most of them don't even engage in that classic CEO pastime: golf.' There's no opportunity. The CEO spends a goodly proportion of time simply in transit, a fashion both risky and irksome. Chris Jones of advertising giant J. Walter Thompson resigned in January 2001 after suffering deep vein thrombosis on a flight from New York to Geneva. A dig of BHP Billiton directors when they ousted Brian Gilbertson in January 2003 was that he was 'always on a plane'.

The CEO's relationship to money, meanwhile, is complex. Practically, money means little to him. He has more than he will ever need, and in the course of an average day will spend little of his own: the company charge card caters for quotidian needs; a cheap corporate loan covers anything more elaborate. Yet financial security seems to breed personal insecurities, which mutate into gnawing questions: 'How much am I earning?' 'How much is he earning?' 'Why aren't I earning as much as him?' Daniel Vasella, the CEO of the Swiss drug giant Novartis, confessed a couple of years ago to have gone through a stage of blinding obsession with his rewards: 'The strange part is, the more I made, the more I got preoccupied with money. When suddenly I didn't have to think about money as much, I found myself thinking increasingly about it.' So much for the theory of money's instrumentality, that it is useful only for what it can buy. In the executive suite, money confers status; it becomes an abstract indicator of being.

Those who believe regulation and transparency can solve all social ills should acknowledge that their consequence in this instance has been perfectly perverse. More information about CEO salaries was meant to encourage vigilance and curb excess; *au contraire*, vigilance weakened and excess exceeded itself. Bill Flanagan, an editor at *Forbes* and *Businessweek* when they first started to track and tabulate executive pay thirty years ago, sensed the cultural shift in the fading volume of complaints he received:

> In the mid-seventies, public relations people would call me all the time, complaining that we had overstated their bosses' compensation.... But those complaints faded after a while. CEOs began to realise that it paid to advertise. The information is public anyway – revealed in the company's proxy statement sent to all shareholders. That's where the magazines got their numbers. CEOs felt that if you had a great year, why not flaunt it? They wanted everyone to know how valuable they were.

A concession to the sensibilities of others in the executive lexicon is that 'money' is *anything but*. CEOs these days are seldom 'paid': they are 'compensated', or 'rewarded'. This is odd. Compensation is usually the salve for injury or ordeal; reward generally accrues as an outcome of risk. What injuries do CEOs sustain? What risks do they run? They work long hours: so do many. They might get sacked: so might all. But then, there are many expressions in the executive lexicon with the reek of doublespeak about them. The phrase 'internationally competitive', for instance, has taken on conspicuously divergent meanings where top and bottom of the salary scale are concerned: while workers are enjoined to price their labour to compete with the cheapest rival, CEOs seek convergence with the highest common denominator.

Money *does* buy things, and in *extremis* their acquisition can become compulsive. Dennis Kozlowski, whose Tyco International at its peak was worth more than Ford, General Motors and Daimler Chrysler put together, has become as notorious for his taste as his takings: his $6000 shower curtain,

$15,000 dog-shaped umbrella standard, $2200 gilded wastebasket, and $2.1 million birthday party for his wife in Sardinia, featuring singer Jimmy Buffett and an ice sculpture of Michelangelo's David that dispensed Stolichnaya through its appendage. Hearings at the Royal Commission investigating the collapse of Australia's biggest insurance company, HIH, disclosed a comparable squandermania in Ray Williams, who bestowed Cuban cigars worth A$1600 on a favourite debtor, dispensed A$7000 Baume and Mercier gold watches to staff, and in one fortnight spent as much as A$9000 at a veritable Michelin Guide of restaurants. These items, though, were not merely about being rich: for Kozlowski and Williams, the *coup* lay in leading their baroque lifestyles at company expense.

The CEO, then, is not simply another 'conspicuous consumer', but a 'conspicuous earner'. And the earnings come not purely from contracted emoluments, bonuses, stock and golden gimmies, but in the appurtenances of office: the top-floor office eyrie, the limousine, the personal assistant, the entertainment budget and that modern equivalent of Cleopatra's barge, the executive jet. A new trend is rewards for the CEO's family circle: the nearest, as it were, of the dearest. The pay package settled in 2003 on William Aldinger III, CEO of HSBC offshoot Household International, included lifetime dental care for him and his wife; the rewards for Lloyds TSB's new CEO Eric Daniels include the payment of school fees for his children; when defunct telco Global Crossing recruited AT & T's Robert Annunziata five years ago, his pot included first-class air travel for his mother.

In its reliance on perquisites, the management of the modern corporation is reminiscent of the *ancien régime,* where de Tocqueville found each group 'differentiated from the rest by its right to petty privileges, even the least of which was regarded as a token of its exalted status'. And by the time you are a CEO, the privileges are far from petty. Even the corporate HQ can be thought of as a form of gratification, of ego if not of income. No wonder so many bosses down the years have invested so extravagantly in head offices. And no wonder it has often foredoomed them, like the Sears Roebuck Tower, which as a monument to its boss's self-regard attracted the epithet 'Gordon Metcalf's Last Erection', and English Electric's palatial pile on the site of the Aldwych's Gaiety Theatre, commissioned by its hereditary chairman Lord Nelson, furnished 'like a miniature Versailles', and auctioned off without hesitation when the company was swallowed by rival General Electric.

Soldiers of
Fortune Magazine

$$\$\$\$$

How are we to imagine the CEO at work? It has stretched more than a few minds. Peter Drucker, the progenitor of management gurudom, likened myth-making about the executive suite to 'the medieval geographer's picture of Africa as a stamping ground of the one-eyed ogre, the immortal phoenix and the elusive unicorn'. The tendency is to lapse into tropes made familiar by leaders in other fields. The CEO is commonly seen as kin to the field-marshal hovering over an ordnance map in his chateau and barking orders at his general staff while pushing tin soldiers here and toy cannons there. And strangely, while most management thinkers would now dismiss this picture as archaic, it contains a kernel of truth. Ideas of hierarchy and strategy in corporations are direct transpositions from the military. When management education began, in fact, where was one to look but the armed forces? Bethlehem Iron Company's founder Joseph Wharton told students in 1890 that the business school named in his honour would 'instil a sense of the coming strife' in which each manager would be 'a soldier'. As John Kay has also noted, the connection is, well... kinda cool: 'What boy (and most chief executives are men) has not dreamt of destroying his opponents with his new technology or his ingenuity? What youth has not identified with the great field generals of history... inspiring their men to heroic feats with a few well-chosen words of encouragement and inspiration?' Thus the free indulgence in military metaphor by CEOs from Lee Iacocca ('I was the general in the war to save Chrysler') to Larry Ellison ('My ideal vice-president would be Genghis Khan'), not to mention *delenda est Carthago* mission statements like Nike's 'Crush Adidas', Kohmatsu's 'Encircle Caterpillar', Kao's 'KPG' ('Kill Procter & Gamble') and Honda's 'Yamaha Wo Tsubusu!' ('We will crush, squash, slaughter Yamaha!').

This metaphor, however, has obvious limits. 'Force and fraud are in war the two cardinal virtues,' said Thomas Hobbes – and, strange as it may seem, they aren't in business. Nor is business a zero-sum game. Success derives from your creation, not others' destruction. And business, Kay has observed, should never encourage valour:

> Military history abounds with stories of heroism in the face of adversity – Horatio defending the bridge, Custer's last stand, the charge of the Light Brigade.... But if General Custer or Lord Raglan had been businessmen, we should not have wished to have been their employees or to have bought their shares, and I would not myself have wished to invest in Horatio either. Fighting against overwhelming odds may sometimes be necessary military strategy. It is almost never a sensible business strategy.

Drucker himself originated a popular metaphor: the CEO as conductor, combining the activities of many talented individuals in a common purpose. Again this has its virtues. Like the conductor, the CEO is there not simply to provide direction, but to satisfy the human longing for a single visible figurehead. But again, the metaphor's limitations are little less obvious. Orchestras look a good deal more similar to each other than do companies; it is not in a conductor's remit to sell out of strings, spend the proceeds on more percussion, and replace the piano with a Moog synthesiser. More illuminating, perhaps, are the curious parallels between the rises of the conductor and the CEO as recognisable models of leadership. Conducting as a specialist activity began when composers abdicated directing their own scores, just as salaried bosses moved in when entrepreneurs began stepping back from daily involvement in the enterprises they'd founded. Conducting and management being portable skills about which there is abiding magic and mystery, a tiny elite in both now flit from job to job fetching outsized fees; one is sometimes reminded, when looking at the many foreigners now in charge of FTSE-100 companies, of Sir Thomas Beecham's gripe: 'Why do we have so many third-rate foreign conductors round when we have so many second-rate ones of our own?' The implications of paralleling the occupations are especially intriguing when it is considered that, strictly speaking, conductors are not integral to the performance of classical music. As one distinguished practitioner, Daniel Barenboim, has conceded: 'Orchestral conducting as a full-time occupation is an invention – a sociological not an artistic one – of the twentieth century.' To quote the heretical critic Hans Keller: 'The conductor's existence is, essentially, superfluous, and you have to attain a high degree of musical stupidity in order to find watching the beat, or the conductor's inane face for that matter, easier for the purpose of knowing when and how to play than simply listening to the music.' New York's wonderful Orpheus Chamber Orchestra proves the point by going conductorless – 'We don't need someone waving their arms for us to understand a phrase,' stated its founder Julius Feifer – and in a subtle compliment and riposte to Drucker has been the subject of a management book, *Leadership Ensemble* (2001). We await the first CEOless corporation.

It may be better to forget the metaphors and regard the

role of CEO as *sui generis*. Which is not to say it is more exotic than we can imagine; if anything, it is more prosaic. Still perhaps the best guide is Henry Mintzberg's *The Nature of Managerial Work* (1973). Having spent time with five CEOs in different industries, and surveyed the contents of a sizeable sample of management diaries, Mintzberg concluded that the traditional roles of planning, organisation, coordination and control had little bearing on executive routines. Only ten per cent of the boss's activities took more than an hour:

> The chief executives met a steady stream of callers and mail from the moment they arrived in the morning until they left in the evening.... A diary study of 160 British top and middle managers found that they worked for half an hour or more without interruption about once every two days. The traditional literature notwithstanding, the job of managing does not breed reflective planners; the manager responds to stimuli as an individual who is conditioned by his job to prefer live to delayed action.

The fragmentation of the executive's time, Mintzberg found, was strangely intrinsic to his stimulation:

> Jumping from topic to topic, he thrives on interruptions and, more often than not, disposes of items in ten minutes or less. Though he may have fifty projects going, all are delegated. He juggles them, checking each one periodically before sending it back into orbit.

Mintzberg's subjects, he concluded, were indistinguishable from their counterparts of 100 years earlier: 'The information they need differs, but they seek it in the same way; by word of mouth. Their decisions concern modern technology, but the procedures they use are still the same as the procedures of the nineteenth century.' Much, of course, has changed in thirty years, though one's impressions are generally that more has meant worse. 'As yet, there seems to be no modern equivalent to Mintzberg's research,' comments Carol Kennedy in her recent survey of management thought *The Next Big Thing* (2000). 'It's a safe bet that the results would be even more unsettling.' Mintzberg, an accomplished phrase-maker, has since likened management to sex, in that 'you are supposed to figure it out but nobody tells you what to do'. Which, it should be said, suits some. Jack Welch relished his job's disorder:

> Being a CEO is the nuts! A whole jumble of thoughts come to mind: Over the Top. Wild. Fun. Outrageous. Crazy. Passions. Perpetual motion. The give-and-take. Meetings into the night. Incredible friendships. Fine wine. Celebrations. Great golf courses. Big decisions in the real game. Crises and pressure. Lots of swings. A few home runs. The thrill of winning. The pain of losing. It's as good as it gets!

Up to a point, Lord Welch. If you're turning over a subject every ten minutes, how effective can you be? Even improved information technology is a mixed blessing for the modern CEO. He knows more, in terms of real-time intelligence from market frontiers – what's selling, what's not, who's gaining, who's slipping behind. But he also knows less – such specialist knowledge as he had begins at once to slip out of date, and his dependence on the expertise of others grows. Frankly, the company makes profits in ways he barely understands. It is hard to forget the touchingly ingenuous comment of Peter Baring recorded in the minutes of an informal Bank of England consultation in September 1993: 'The recovery in profitability has been amazing following the reorganisation, leaving Barings to conclude that it was not actually terribly difficult to make money in the securities business.' The eponymous 230-year-old bank founded by his forbears had at that stage sixteen months of independent existence left.

If there is a new dimension to the CEO's role, it is that

introduced by the demands of the investment and media communities in a media-saturated age: that of shaper of perceptions. This appears to be a generational shift. Jack Welch did not know who the CEO of General Electric was for his first ten years at the company; when he was CEO, there was never any risk he would fail for want of exposure. Again, though, this is in some respects the continuation and intensification of an old phenomenon. Bosses have always had public and private faces. In Thomas Mann's mighty novel of a Hanseatic business dynasty *Buddenbrooks* (1901), Thomas Buddenbrook is acutely conscious of the strain of keeping up appearances: 'No doubt of it – Thomas Buddenbrook's existence was no different from that of an actor, but one whose whole life has become a single production, down to the smallest, most workaday detail – a production that... constantly engaged and devoured all his energies.' The only character who intuits his struggle is his otherwise ineffectual son Hanno, who is filled with foreboding by watching his father place and replace a mask of calm for each business encounter:

> Not only did he see his father's poise and charm and their effect on everyone, but his strange, stinging, perceptive glance saw how terribly difficult it was for his father to bring it off, how after each visit he grew more silent and pale.... Hanno knew that they all expected him to appear in public someday, too, and to perform, to prepare each word and gesture, with everyone staring at him – and at the thought, he closed his eyes with a shudder of fear and aversion.

The difference today is in the scale and science of the CEO's image rather than its essence. And the task of what we might call managing outward, as distinct from managing inward, is both as significant and insignificant as perceptions are inclined to be, for while the two are often mistaken, the former is no substitute for the latter. Preoccupation with the market's demands, in fact, tends to foster the delusion that crises are merely matters of perception that with good PR can be 'managed'. As Enron approached its final reckoning, for example, Ken Lay lambasted not banks, rivals, investors or employees, but his corporate communications department: 'This is a public relations problem. Why can't you solve it?' When Al Dunlap faced serious criticism for the first time in his career at Sunbeam, he fired a succession of public relations advisers. 'They're beating the shit out of me,' he complained. 'We're taking the punches and I'm not a guy who takes punches. People who believe in me are wondering if something is wrong because I'm not responding.... I've got to get out there.' In there, though, the damage had already been done.

So these developments are both new and not new: the CEO's has always been an awkward role, of power and helplessness, of presence and absence. He makes decisions, but delegates most of their implementation. He knows things, but mostly what others, with superior knowledge of their respective areas better, tell him. He builds an image, but it's... well, an image. One of the most considered summaries of CEO life is 'The Dilemma of Corporation Man' by J. Irwin Miller, forty years the chief of Cummins Engine of Columbus, Indiana. A Rhodes scholar who studied philosophy and played the violin, Miller became so famous for his philanthropy and liberalism that he made it onto Richard Nixon's 'enemies list'. But as he explained in *Fortune* in August 1959, his job filled him with humility, and sometimes despair:

> To illustrate, let us suppose we can see inside the head of the president of a large manufacturing organisation. His

34

company employs 20,000 people and operates half a dozen plants. It distributes its products in every state and in many foreign countries, and – most frightening of all – it has competitors. Now let us suppose that these competitors are extremely vigorous, and that our president knows that to maintain his share of the market and to make earnings which will please his directors, he must accomplish the following very quickly: design and perfect a brand-new and more advanced line of products; tool up these products in such a way as to permit higher quality and lower costs than his competitors; purchase new machinery; arrange major additional long-term financing. At the same time, his corporation's labor contract is up for negotiation, and this must be rewritten in such a way as to obtain good employee response and yet make no more concessions than do his competitors. Sales coverage of all customers has to be intensified, and sales costs reduced. Every one of these objectives must be accomplished simultaneously, and ahead of similar efforts on the part of his competitors – or the future of the company is in great danger. Every head of a corporation lives every day with the awareness that it is quite possible to go broke. At the same time he lives with the awareness that he cannot possibly accomplish a single one of these objectives. The actual work will have to be accomplished by numerous individuals, some actually unknown to him, most of them many layers removed from his direct influence in the organisation. It is because of this the president becomes frantic.... He becomes dogmatic. He issues orders. He says things are jolly well going to be done this way and no other. He says the company's negotiators are not to give in on the union's demands for premium pay or the union shop. He says every salesman must make so many calls each day. He says you can't add a single person to this office, which has already got too many people in it. And he pounds the table every time he says these things. For he feels that this great, vast and ponderous organisation is his enemy and that inside its faceless exteri-

or all his plans, his programs, his timetables will be diluted, slowed down, and ultimately defeated. Success seems to him to have come only in rare instances, and to have been of a temporary and ephemeral nature. He thinks of himself as being in a race that has no finish line. And his real antagonist is neither the customer, nor his bankers, nor the union. His real antagonist is the organisation.

The current debate about the role and renown of CEOs, then, seems one-dimensional – in its fixation with the CEO's control of corporations, it overlooks the degree to which the corporation controls its CEO. It will be the argument of this book that paying outsized sums to CEOs is not simply socially offensive but intellectually difficult to justify – for reasons, moreover, inseparable from the development and character of the corporation itself.

Past Masters
of the Universe

$$$

The modern industrial corporation is the slow-ripened fruit of centuries, with origins stretching back to the Renaissance. It was made possible chiefly by three developments: the financial innovation of double-entry book-keeping, which allowed a separation between individuals and their commercial activities; the structural concept of the joint-stock company, pooling the resources of a group of investors and answerable to a board of directors; and the legal idea of limited liability. Of these, the third is perhaps most important to our story. Before limited liability, a person who had invested either individually or in partnership risked their whole worth: debtors' prisons were full of inadvertent and honourable failures. Few outside the founders and their kin would buy shares unless they either knew the firm's principals personally or could otherwise monitor its doings. Under limited liability – first permitted on restricted bases in the early nineteenth century – stockholders could not be held liable for the corporation's misdeeds. At the dawn of capitalism, firms had been run by founders and, if they lasted that long, their heirs. By relieving shareholders of the need for unwavering vigilance, limited liability explicitly foresaw firms outliving their first generation under the guidance of a new class: the salaried manager.

Much like modern parents anguishing about the theory and practice of childcare, owners experienced pangs about entrusting their enterprises to hirelings. Charles Dickens dramatised their unease in *Dombey and Son* (1848). For all his later Bounderbys, Gradgrinds and Merdles, Dickens created no business relationship quite so intriguing as that between capitalist Paul Dombey, who thinks he is in charge of his firm of merchants, and manager James Carker, who knows he is. When the novel opens, Paul Dombey is at his peak:

> The earth was made for Dombey and Son to trade in and the sun and moon were made to give them light. Rivers and seas were formed to float their ships; rainbows gave them promise of fair weather; winds blew for or against their enterprises' stars and planets circled in their orbits, to preserve inviolate a system of which they were the centre.

When this 'colossus of commerce' speaks, the world listens. His most famous speech, to his son, extols the virtues of wealth: 'Money, Paul, can do anything.... ' Yet it has not acquired him the loyalty of Carker, 'sly of manner, sharp of tooth, soft of foot, watchful of eye, oily of tongue, cruel of heart, nice of habit'. When Dombey is distracted by his son's death, Carker uses his absences to 'explore the mysteries of books and papers, with the patient progress of a man who was dissecting the minutest nerves and fibres of his subject', constructing 'a labyrinth of which only he held the clue'. Having sedulously scuttled the business, Carker then takes off with Dombey's second wife, though not before pouring out to his brother a timeless lament of the embittered manager:

> There is not a man employed here, standing between myself and the lowest in place... who wouldn't be glad at

heart to see his master humbled: who does not hate him, secretly: who does not wish him evil rather than good: and who would not turn upon him, if he had the power and boldness. The nearer to his favour, the nearer to his insolence, the closer to him, the farther from him. That's the creed here! ... Bah! There's not one among them, but if he had at once the power, and the wit and daring to use it, would not scatter Dombey's pride and lay it low, as ruthlessly as I rake out these ashes.

Dombey and Son was a strikingly subtle conception of where business had been and was headed with ownership and control decisively separated. Carker's death beneath a locomotive's wheels is even symbolically apt; it would be in American railyards, junctions, stations and sidings later that century that the manager first took advantage of his empowerment. While the 'Gilded Age', roughly from the end of the Civil War to the turn of the century, is popularly associated with the regnancy of Wall Street and the kleptocracy of Vanderbilts, Goulds, Drews and Fisks, railways also demanded more managers: managers more dispersed and more autonomous, observing controls, policies, corporate structures and reporting lines.

As often occurs, it required a crisis for an awareness of need to dawn. In his 'Report on Avoiding Collisions and Governing the Employees' following a collision in October 1841 on the Boston & Worcester Railroad, investigating engineer George Whistler saw the solution in 'drawing solid lines of authority and communication for the railroad's administration, maintenance and operation'. The line was divided into three contiguous operating divisions, each with an assistant master of transportation reporting to the board, roadmaster, senior mechanic and foreman. These ideas caught on. Erie Railroad's general superintendent Daniel McCallum had a particularly elaborate vision, harnessing the new-fangled telegraph to collect hourly reports from super-intendents of geographic sections, and daily bulletins from conductors, agents and engineers. *American Railroad Journal* found his pioneering organisational diagram so mind-boggling that it offered lithographed copies for $1. But the ablest manager – and really the first CEO as we would understand it – was J. Edgar Thomson. Pennsylvania Railroad, of which he was president and chairman, was the first big organisation run by management on behalf of a mostly passive group of investors. An engineer who began his career as a rodman in a survey crew, Thomson presided over an expansion of Pennsylvania's network from 250 miles to 6000 miles, and diversifications into mining its own coal, making its own steel, and running its own steamships between London and Philadelphia. Most importantly, he honeycombed the Pennsylvania with managers, including a head office with discrete operating, accounting, treasury and legal departments. At its zenith in the early 1890s the Pennsylvania employed 110,000 people – America's army and navy ran to fewer than 40,000. 'We are specialists,' gushed a colleague. 'That is, pygmies. Thomson was great in everything – operating, traffic, motive power, finance; but most important of all in organisation.'

However large commercial organisations seem today, their proportional scale at the turn of the century was greater still. When J. P. Morgan brokered the creation of US Steel in July 1901, it was capitalised at $1.4 billion, while the whole of the American manufacturing was worth only $9 billion. US Steel employed 168,000, controlled 1600km of rail, 112 ore carriers, smelted 65 per cent of American steel and extracted half its iron ore. Yet to call it a corporation in the modern sense would be a misnomer: it was the holding company for an aggregation of entities, and would be bedevilled for decades by its internal incoherence. In broad and simple terms, business and its leadership moved into the future in three iterations, embodied in individuals who were perhaps history's three foremost industrialists: John D. Rockefeller, Henry Ford and Alfred Sloan.

A grab of elementary economics may be helpful here. Business knows two ways to expand. The first is horizontal combination: buying rivals to reduce competition. This became a vogue in America's depression of the 1870s, when railroads responded to excess capacity and deflation by forming industry associations and cartels to fix rates among themselves. Thus what is known colloquially as the rise of the all-powerful trust in the commercial affairs of the United States; thus, too, the emergence of Rockefeller, in real terms still history's wealthiest individual. Hailing from Cleveland, at the terminus of railroads stretching from Pennsylvania's newly opened Oil Regions, Rockefeller was a trader in pork, grain and other staples who invested in a couple of refineries and a cooperage operation, and who rather than peeling away to count his cash after his first fortune remained to make many more. Standard Oil, established in January 1870, assumed its name to emphasise its products' uniform quality, but also set standards for business, both in management expertise and in minatory bulk. Rampaging across the Oil Regions throughout the 1870s, Rockefeller 'horizontally combined' about 90 per cent of America's refining capacity into a giant trust, consolidated by the Standard Oil Trust Agreement of January 1882.

Rockefeller then seized on what's now understood as the second method of business expansion: vertical integration, the acquisition of suppliers and customers to reduce costs. Standard moved from refining into distribution by buying pipelines, then tackled marketing, and finally exploration. Perhaps no enterprise in history has been so self-contained.

Because the only commercial men Rockefeller despised as much as bankers were brokers, Standard Oil was funded almost entirely from retained earnings. And as Rockefeller believed in 'uncovering no surface unnecessarily', trust headquarters was an unmarked greystone building at 26 Broadway in Lower Manhattan described chillingly in Thomas Lawson's period classic *Frenzied Finance* (1906): 'Solid as a prison, towering as a steeple, its cold and forbidding facade seemed to rebuke the heedless levity of the passing crowd, and frown on the frivolity of the stray sunbeams which in the late afternoon played round its impassive cornices.'

Rockefeller, however, proved himself a unique hybrid – as his biographer Ron Chernow has expressed it: 'both the instinctive, first-generation entrepreneur who founds a company and the analytic second-generation manager who extends and develops it'. Standard's executive committee convened daily at noon. Rockefeller left the head of the table to the group's oldest member, Charles Pratt, and favoured consensus: 'Our general rule was to take no important action till all of us were convinced of its wisdom.' Some controls were strict: all expenditures above $5000 and salary increases above $50 a month required top-level approval. But other matters were devolved to a group of sub-committees – transportation, production, pipelines, domestic trade, export trade, manufacturing, purchasing, case and can, cooperage and others – served by a permanent secretariat consisting of eleven staff departments. Standard Oil's management corps, Lawson thought, were as drilled and disciplined as an army: 'Every Standard Oil man must wear the "Standard Oil collar". This collar is riveted to each one as he is taken into "the band", and can only be removed with the head of the wearer.' Rockefeller espoused a commercial creed of the utmost rationality: 'Real efficiency in work comes from knowing your facts and building upon that sure foundation.' Standard Oil was built in his own image. Even Rockefeller's muckraker nemesis Ida Tarbell had to admit: 'There was not a lazy bone in the organisation, not an incompetent hand, nor a stupid head.'

'Down with all tyrants!' shouts a character in Eugene O'Neill's *A Moon for the Misbegotten* (1947). 'Goddamn Standard Oil!' God, though, eventually had nothing to do with the eclipse of the Standard Oil and its trust brethren: rather was it Teddy Roosevelt, whose Bureau of Corporations in February 1902 took the first of forty-four anti-trust actions in his seven-year presidency. Yet Roosevelt was too shrewd to try throwing the Gilded Age completely into reverse; he restrained himself even amid his famous 1907 damnation of 'the malefactors of great wealth' at the Gridiron Club: 'I believe in corporations. They are indispensable instruments of our modern civilisation; but I believe that they should be so supervised and so regulated that they shall act for the interests of the community as a whole.' And in some respects, believes Alfred Chandler, the Herodotus of business history, Roosevelt's trust-busters actually accelerated the creation of big enterprises: the only way to avoid being regarded as one of those sinister associations, cartels, trusts or holding companies was to consolidate completely – to become, in other words, a giant corporation.

To the drive for dominance would henceforward be harnessed an avidity for efficiency. It had been a dream of the industrial revolution, as expressed by Josiah Wedgwood, to 'make such machines of men as cannot err'. This became the obsession of an American statistician, Frederick Winslow Taylor, whose approach was to decompose a job into its simplest activities, reduce the time required by each, and find the 'one best way' of fulfilling a job; the stopwatch-toting Taylorist manager has been a bogey of liberals and trade unionists ever since. This is ironic, for the 'scientific management' revolution at the beginning of the twentieth century won its first ardent advocates among those who wished to make business more accountable, not less. Taylor's first public proselyte was a prominent democrat, the eminent American jurist Louis Brandeis, aka 'the People's Lawyer', who in August 1910 challenged the Pennsylvania, New York Central and Baltimore & Ohio Railroads in the Federal Trade Commission to justify a hike in freight rates. When they claimed that 'practice, contact and experience' justified their decision – NYC's vice-president Charles Daly opined memorably that 'the basis of my judgement is exactly the same as the basis of a man who knows how to play a good game of golf' – Brandeis brandished a copy of Taylor's pioneering *Shop Management* (1903). If business ran along 'scientific' lines, Brandeis believed, its freedom to wield market power capriciously and arbitrarily would be circumscribed.

It is hard to believe that the eerily totalitarian tone of *The Principles of Scientific Management* (1911) ever warmed the cockles of a liberal's heart: 'In the past, man has been first. In the future the System must be first.' But many agreed, and none more wholeheartedly than Detroit's pioneering carmaker Henry Ford. No scholar has linked Taylor and Ford directly – Taylor ridiculed Ford's 'very cheaply and roughly made' Model T, while Ford's rudimentary education would have been stretched by Taylor's tangled prose – but they were cultural kin. Ford's notion of assembly-line mass-production methods was labour divided and conquered. 'Both Taylor and Ford raised production, cut costs – and reduced the judgement and skill needed by the average worker,' says Robert Kanigel, Taylor's biographer. 'After Ford and Taylor, most jobs needed less of everything – less brains, less muscle, less independence.' They also produced more of everything.

Detroit's Highland Park, at which the assembly line was finally applied to the production of whole cars in October 1913, was seen by Rockefeller as 'the industrial miracle of the age'. By 1920, Ford was producing a car a minute; by 1925, a car every ten seconds.

Ford challenged the mores of American commerce in another equally important way, by seeing advantage in what he could do rather than in the prevention of what others might. 'I found that competition was supposed to be a menace and that a good manager circumvented his competitors by getting a monopoly through artificial means,' recalled Ford. 'The idea was that there were only a certain number of people who could buy and that it was necessary to get their trade ahead of someone else.' Ford expanded his business, instead, by building the market. His stated objective was to build a car that 'no man making a good salary will be unable to own and enjoy' – and from January 1914 he also provided the good salary by paying workers $5 a day. The *Wall Street Journal* disdained 'the most foolish thing ever attempted in the industrial world', which had injected 'spiritual principles into a field where they do not belong'. Ford retorted piously that it was 'a plain act of social justice'. Neither was right: Ford's initiative was principally to counter staff turnover, which by December 1913 had reached 380 per cent (Ford, in other words, was hiring 963 men to keep 100). But the reasons mattered little: 10,000 stormed the gate clamouring for work the day after the policy was announced. Ford had at a stroke begotten his own customers. No single gesture in industrial history marked more clearly the transformation of an age of scarcity into one of abundance.

When Ford commissioned his River Rouge works at Dearborn after the First World War – ninety-three buildings connected by 149km of railroad and 43km of conveyor belts employing 75,000 men – he appeared to have brought industry to a peak of vertically-integrated perfection. It had its own power plant, iron forges, fabricating facilities – even its own pulp mill and sheep run, producing respectively the paper for stationery and the wool for the Model T's seat covers. 'If absolute completeness and perfect adaptation of means to end justify the word,' said J. A. Spender, 'they are in their own way works of art.' Ford's *My Life and Work* (1923) was devoured by everyone from Konosuke Matsushita, Japan's first significant industrialist, to Bertrand Russell and Bernard Shaw. It went through thirty editions in Germany, where Hitler was an admirer, and became popular in Russia, where its translators reached the somewhat surprising conclusion that 'Fordism is a system the principles of which have been known for long, [having been] laid down by Marx.' Lenin campaigned for 'the teaching of the Taylor system and its systematic trial and adaptation' and Stalin placed Ford's architects, the brothers Kahn, in charge of his design bureau during the First Five-Year Plan ('the Great Leap Forward'). A Ford tractor plant was made the centrepiece of the industrial precinct in Stalin's new Volga city, Stalingrad.

Seldom, however, has a public figure trashed their reputation so conscientiously. Even overlooking the assembly line's dehumanising propensities – and Ford candidly conceded his conviction that 'a great business is really too big to be human' – his deeds and dicta feature something to offend everybody, from his beastly maltreatment of his son and the prickly praetorian guard he maintained at River Rouge to his purse-mouthed disgust with shareholders and anti-Semitic outpourings in the *Dearborn Independent*. And, for all his genius as a manufacturer, Ford was an abject failure as a manager, abhorring all aspects of business bar production: 'There is no bent of mind more dangerous than that which is described as the "genius for organisation". And so the Ford factories have no organisation, no specific duties attaching to any position, no line of succession or of authority.' He steadily alienated his closest allies, sacked his ablest manufacturers and salesmen, and prohibited the most basic bureaucratic functions, one day capriciously firing all the company's accountants. 'They're not productive,' he railed. 'They don't do any real work. I want them out of here today.' The company became like a powerful engine harnessed to a driverless shell, for Ford also forbade any change to his dear but dour Model T. When he finally discontinued the marque in March 1927, he simply closed the factory, only then commencing design of its successor. 'If there is any certainty as to what a businessman is,' observed John Kenneth Galbraith, 'he is assuredly the things Ford was not.' By the onset of the Great Depression, the avatar of the assembly line had been eclipsed: 'Mr Ford, who had so many brilliant insights in earlier years, seemed never to understand how completely the market had changed from the one in which he had made his name and to which he was accustomed.' The writer of these deferential lines, Alfred M. Sloan, would be business's glass of fashion for fully half a century.

The Sloan Age

$$$

No company has made a better acquisition. Alfred Sloan joined General Motors when his Hyatt Roller Bearing Company was purchased in July 1916. But GM, a holding company of automotive businesses gathered by a crazy-brave entrepreneur called William Durant, was at the time in more or less constant upheaval. Sloan admired Durant's 'automotive genius, his imagination, his generous human qualities and his integrity', but 'thought he was too casual in his ways for an administrator, and he overloaded himself'. Sloan's response when Durant finally lost his job after an automotive market slump in September 1920, levered out by its biggest shareholder Du Pont, was to institute what Peter Drucker has called 'the first deliberate attempt to organise the modern large industrial enterprise', combining Rockefeller's zeal for organisation with Ford's passion for production.

With the patronage of Durant's successor Pierre Du Pont, scion of the great chemicals firm, Sloan diagnosed GM's most recent prostration as the outcome of poor information. Output had been increased despite a six-month timelag on sales data, allowing inventory to blow out. Production schedules would henceforward be regularised by head office, based on figures from dealers collected every ten days and monthly information on car registrations. Sloan also believed in the most rigorous financial controls, and in January 1921 obtained from Du Pont Corporation an outstanding account- ant, F. Donaldson Brown, who had dreamed up such exotic ideas as 'turnover', and 'return on investment'. Applying these ideas at GM, Sloan originated the Nelsonian epigram: 'Every dollar must make a showing for itself.'

As he built this centre, Sloan proceeded more or less simultaneously with a scheme known as 'decentralisation'. As classically delineated by Nobel laureate Ronald Coase, the rationale for the large corporation is that combining activi- ties in a single entity lowers 'transactional costs': the expens- es incurred in matching buyers and sellers, negotiating prices, and finalising contracts. The problem is that large organisations also tend toward diseconomies of scale. There are agency costs, where the firm develops a stake in its own survival, and information costs, when managers lose track of what's happening. There is also the problem of the 'free rider': the larger an organisation becomes, the greater the tendency for individuals to slacken off, failing to contribute their fair share to the common weal. The objective, then, is paradoxical: a corporation should be as big as it has to be, and as small as it can be.

Sloan resolved these tensions by envisioning a multidi- visional firm overlain by a head office controlling func- tions such as strategy, treasury and research, and reporting to executive and finance committees which answered in their turn to directors. 'I do not regard size as a barrier,' he asserted. 'To me it is only a problem of management.' In a memo that stands to evolution of the corporation as Luther's ninety-five theses stand to the Reformation, Sloan contended that 'decentralisation' would improve organisa- tional morale 'by placing each operation on its own foun- dation', permit the collection of financial data 'correctly reflecting the relation between the net return and the invested capital of each operating division', and enable GM to 'direct the placing of additional capital where it will result in the greatest benefit to the corporation as a whole'. Sloan's idea wasn't entirely original: both Du Pont Corporation and Germany's Siemens had explored similar structures. But he was bolder. Where they were controlled by owner-managers, GM resembled the old Pennsylvania Railroad in being run by salarymen. GM's car divisions, furthermore, were demarcated along product lines, each with a specific demographic in mind: 'a car for every purse and purpose', in the famous formulation, with 'Chevrolet for the hoi polloi, Pontiac for the poor but proud, Oldsmobile for the comfortable but discreet, Buick for the striving, Cadillac for the rich'. GM, in Sloan's aphorism, did not make automobiles, but money.

Sloan was avowedly a leader, seeking explicitly 'to centralise the control of all the executive functions of the corporation in the President as its chief executive officer'. He later forced the resignations of Pierre Du Pont and executive committee member John Raskob when they joined the anti-prohibition movement, explaining: 'General Motors is not in politics. It will not permit its prestige, its organisation, or its property to be used for political purposes.' But notice that 'it': Sloan was also determined to depersonalise management, to create a firm that was not beholden to the impulses of a messianic individual like a Durant or a Ford. When *Fortune* studied Sloan at work with his executives in 1938, he was glimpsed in association rather than isolation:

> In this committee work Mr Sloan displays an almost inhuman detachment from personalities, a human and infectious enthusiasm for the facts. Never in committee or out does he give an order in the ordinary sense, saying 'I want you to do this'. Rather he reviews the data and then sells an idea, pointing out what could be done. Brought to consider

the facts in open discussion, all men, he feels, are on an
equal footing. Management is no longer a matter of taking
orders, but of taking counsel.

It was thirty years since Ambrose Bierce had defined a 'corporation' as 'an ingenious device for obtaining individual
profit without individual responsibility'. Sloan had now vin-
dicated an earlier lexicographer, Dr Johnson, who believed
that 'wit can stand its ground against truth only a little
while'. The modern industrial corporation, consolidated into
a single entity but redefined along divisional lines, run by a
hierarchy of salaried managers reporting to a board and
CEO, had arrived – and has never really left. If you can set
aside your ideological *parti pris* for a moment, you might
even salute it as the most important invention of the twentieth century. You might also wonder why you have, in all
likelihood, not heard of Alfred Sloan. The straightforward
answer is that much as we enjoy bandying round words like
'capitalism' and 'globalisation', we prefer to regard them as
impersonal forces synonymous with exploitation, rather
than as works of human individuals. But the other reason for
Sloan's anonymity is that he sought it. GM eclipsed Ford's
market share in 1932 and never looked back. During the
Second World War, its employee numbers grew to half a million, its sales to $12 billion; a decade later it was the first
corporation to net profits of more than $1 billion. Yet Sloan
remained strikingly obscure: he left no private papers, says
biographer David Farber, because 'his life was so interwoven
with GM that he couldn't separate his affairs from those of
the corporation'.

American business mores were spreading. The entrepreneur Harry Gordon Selfridge who opened his grand Oxford
Street department store in March 1909 espoused capitalism
with a missionary zeal:

People must be governed, and there must be those who govern. Laws must be made, and there must be those who study, and those who execute the laws. People must be taught, and there must be teachers. All these, and the church, the newspaper, the theatre, the fine arts are essential to the completeness of the state, to the happiness and safety of its people; but commerce is the main stem, or trunk, where they are all branches, supplied with the sap of its far-reaching wealth. It is as necessary to the existence to any nation and blood to the physical man. That country in which trade flourishes is accounted happy while that in which commerce droops provokes shaking of heads and prophecies of downfall.

Yet American management was a graft that did not immediately take in Britain, and the growing distances by which British industry fell behind have since given economic historians pause for thought.

Some generalised economic arguments are usually advanced: lack of tariffs, higher wages, the fact that railways had to follow patterns of settlement in Britain, while the opposite applied in the US. But the climacteric can also been viewed as a demonstration that it does matter how a country runs its companies. British firms did not consolidate so readily, either horizontally or vertically. They tended to remain under the control of founders and their families, limiting their available capital, and draining them of dividends at the expense of reinvestment: at the outbreak of the First World War, fully four-fifths of joint stock companies in Britain were still privately owned, and many which weren't were dynastic in nature. Barclays Bank, founded in 1896, was run for decades for the comfort of the founding Bevan, Barclay, Tuke and Tritton families rather than earnings maximisation. Imperial Tobacco, founded in 1901 and at one stage Britain's biggest company, remained until the 1960s essentially a loose-knit confederation of sixteen family businesses with a code of gentlemanly non-competition. British companies were often more imaginative and more interested in off-shore markets, but even the most dynamic displayed little interest in their systems of management. Compare the image of Rockefeller and his collegiate carefully carving up the world with the amiably anarchic style of Marcus and Samuel Samuel at Standard Oil's great British rival Shell:

> The two brothers would always go to the window, their backs to the room, huddled together close, their arms round each other's shoulders, heads bent, talking in low voices, until suddenly they would burst apart in yet another dispute, Mr Sam with loud and furious cries, Mr Marcus speaking softly, but both calling each other fool, idiot, imbecile, until suddenly, for no apparent reason, they were in agreement again. There would be a quick decisive exchange of final views. Then Mr Marcus would say: 'Sam, speak to him on the telephone', and would stand at his brother's shoulder while the telephoning took place.

In general, too, British businessmen did not so much wish to be industrialists as to be rich, and where they were not members of the landed gentry themselves to be on level terms with them. Perhaps surprisingly, Britain's ruling classes proved capable of admitting the *arrivisme*; the upstart bourgeois, however, rather than energizing the aristocracy, became co-opted by the leisure society. A classic example is the thrifty Yorkshireman Tom Spencer who in 1905 quit the eleven-year-old retail venture he had begun with a tenacious Jewish *emigré* called Michael Marks, preferring the life of a gentleman farmer (which he enjoyed for two years before being 'slain by a life of ease'). Marcus Samuel, meanwhile, enjoyed running his oil company, but was more covetous of a country house (acquired in 1895), a title (obtained in 1902, when he became London's Lord Mayor) and an Eton and

Oxford education for his children. His hold over Shell weakened, until he was usurped by Henry Deterding from Holland's Royal Dutch in 1907. Those who stood out of this natural order tended to make everyone a little uncomfortable, like the garrulous Hornblower in John Galsworthy's *The Skin Game* (1920):

> I'm new and ye're an old family. Ye don't like me, ye think
> I'm a pushing man. I go to chapel, and ye don't like that.
> I buy land, and ye don't like that. It threatens the view
> from your windies. Well, I don't like you and I'm not
> going to put up with your attitude. Ye've had things your
> own way too long, and now ye're not going to have them
> any longer.

It was so much easier for everyone if such pushing men found satisfaction in their own nice set of 'windies' like the steel magnate Sir Oswald Coote and his consort in Agatha Christie's *The Seven Dials Mystery* (1921).

> They had lived very happily, first in a couple of rooms, and
> then in a tiny house, and then in a larger house, and then
> in successive houses of increasing magnitude, but always
> within a reasonable distance of 'the Works', until now Sir
> Oswald had reached such an eminence that he and 'the
> Works' were no longer interdependent, and it was his
> pleasure to rent the very largest and most magnificent
> mansions all over England.

The leisure society stood by with its rewards. Sir Oswald has not only rented historic 'Chimneys', but lured its owner, the Marquis of Caterham, onto his board of directors, where he is as decorative but ineffectual as the hood ornament on a Rolls-Royce. As Caterham explains to the inquisitive Bundle Brent:

> He's steel. Steel and iron. He's got the biggest steelworks,
> or whatever you call it, in England. He doesn't, of course,

run the show personally now. It's a company, or companies. He got me in as a director of something or other. Very
good business for me – nothing to do except go down to
the city once or twice a year to one of those hotel places –
Cannon Street or Liverpool Street – and sit round a table
where they have very nice new blotting paper. Then Coote
or some clever Johnny makes a speech simply bristling
with figures, but fortunately you needn't listen to it – and I
can tell you, you often get a jolly good lunch out of it.

In the US, by contrast, not merely was there no aristocracy
per se, but American businessman made an ill fit with the
leisure society. The so-called 'Carnegie Millionaires', for
example, the executives of Carnegie Steel and the other
enterprises who sold their interests to the US Steel combine,
could not conceive of a world without work. Carnegie executive David Garrett Kerr explained:

> Many of them didn't know what to do with their money
> after they got it. There was a reason. They had been
> making steel all their lives. They hadn't much time or
> inclination to go in for outside interests. They hadn't even
> been counting the money they were piling up for them-
> selves. As a consequence, they were amazed when the
> corporation was founded. They found themselves in the
> possession of millions. There was a letdown. All they
> could do was try to devise ways to spend the money that,
> after all, meant nothing to them. As a consequence, many
> of them died comparatively poor. The stockmarket got
> some of them, for they were babes in Wall Street. Poor
> business ventures took away some of their fortunes. Reck-
> less spending and jovial adventures accounted for many
> more millions.

American and British business differed even in their swines.
When the 'vile City ruffian' Augustus Melmotte of Anthony
Trollope's *The Way We Live Now* (1875) succumbed to 'a self-

confidence inspired... by the worship of other men which clouded his intellect', he reached for the prussic acid. When Theodore Dreiser's plutocratic anti-hero Frank Cowperwood was imprisoned in *The Financier* (1912), he was unrepentant. 'I have had my lesson,' he tells himself. 'I am as rich as I was, and only a little older. They caught me once, but they will not catch me again.' Spoken, one might think, like a true CEO.

In one development, however, the stature of the salary-man was enhanced everywhere, and the reach of the individual capitalist checked. The separation of ownership and control, essentially unavoidable since limited liability, was being levered wider by industry's growing scale. Long a feature of American capitalism, the merger spread to Europe. German companies, unconstrained by anti-trust law, had long been wont to form coalitions called *interessengemeinschaften* (communities of interest); now they moved to consolidate further. Chemical giants Bayer, Hoechst and BASF formed IG Farbenindustrie in 1925; a host of German steel companies became Vereinigte Stahlwerke in 1926. Britain's Imperial Chemical Industries was created in a four-way merger the same year, Distillers Company in a six-way merger the following year, and Unilever and Metal Box in other combinations two years later. The railways were reduced to four quasi-monopolies; the banks agglomerated as a big five. The 'successful, emancipated, semi-scientific, and not particularly highbrow businessman' of H. G. Wells' *The World of William Clissold* (1926) prophesied confidently: 'Big business in its increasing quest for efficiency will work steadily and purposefully to eradicate all the faults of our economic organisations which mar the smooth running of the industrial machine.' Even in faraway Australia, home of the merchant venturer and lone prospector, the daily affairs of corporations were increasingly the preserve of professional managers. And without big, greedy, meddlesome owners looking over their shoulders, the likes of Essington Lewis, W. S. Robinson, Colin Fraser and Herbert Gepp found increasing scope for their talents: when Lewis dissuaded BHP's board from installing the costly Duplex steel-making system in February 1921, he was also striking a blow for executive expertise. Like Sloan, Lewis cared little for appearances. When promoted to BHP's board with the title of managing director five years later, his biographer Geoffrey Blainey has noted, Lewis 'shunned the glitter that went with the power; he simply demanded the power'.

As corporations grew so large as to outstrip the capacities of solitary capitalists and even syndicates of investors to own them, observed the pioneering American organisational theorist Mary Parker Follett, the influence of individuals became harder to discern: 'As business is organised today, with its many experts, its planning department, its industrial psychologist, its economic adviser, and its trained managers, the illusion of final responsibility is disappearing.' Corporations were taking on lives of their own. 'The deindividualisation of ownership simultaneously implies the objectification of the thing owned,' said Walter Rathenau, son of and successor to the founder of German electrical giant AEG. 'The claims to ownership are subdivided in such a fashion, and are so mobile, that the enterprise assumes an independent life, as if it belonged to no one.' His words were truer than he knew: his death from an assassin's bullet in 1922 ended family influence at the firm. *Fortune* magazine, founded eight years later, tended to publish 'muscular stories about muscular industries': steel, coal, manufacturing. The individual nominally in charge, where he appeared at all, was an afterthought, and not without reason: by 1938, the average American CEO held just 0.3 per cent of his company's shares.

Alfred Sloan was something of an exception to this. Having swapped his Hyatt Bearing shares for scrip, he was a sizeable GM shareholder. Yet he never saw that role as other than secondary: 'Naturally I like to see GM stock register a good price on the market, but that is just a matter of pride. Personally I consider its price fluctuations inconsequential. What has counted with me is the true value of the property as a business, as an opportunity for the exercise of management talent.' Or lack of talent, as the case might be. For the Sloanist corporation soon attracted critics. The atomisation of ownership, the economists Adolph Berle and Gardiner Means warned darkly in *The Modern Corporation and Private Property* (1932), meant that 'the men in control of a corporation can operate in their own interests, and can divest a portion of the asset fund of income stream to their own uses, such is their privilege'. The lapsed Trotskyist James Burnham, who gave the phenomenon a name in *The Managerial Revolution* (1940), predicted a kind of socialism by stealth: 'In the new structure, when its foundations are completed, there will be no capitalists.' A young economic historian, Peter Drucker, whom GM invited to study its methods, sounded a reproachful note in his *The Concept of the Corporation* (1946): because 'in every large organisation there is a natural tendency to discourage initiative and to put a premium on conformity', big business was destined to suffer 'from parochialism of the executive imagination'.

Yet no one could doubt the profundity of Sloan's influence. It is instanced by another first in his credit: he was the first CEO to appear on *Fortune's* cover. What's notable about this, given that business magazines now rely on CEOs as *Vanity Fair* relies on sleek-headed stars and *Vogue* on airbrushed models, is that it did not happen until September 1963. Even then, the portrait of a pensive Sloan was not to celebrate him as a superman, but to promote a serialisation of his *My Years With General Motors* – a work as bloodless as its appendices, with their column upon column of numbers and page after page of schematic diagrams documenting GM's financial performance and multidivisional structure. It was, as Drucker observed, 'perhaps the most impersonal book of memoirs ever written – and this was clearly intentional'.

The Man Nobody Knows

$$$

A startling aspect of the cult of CEO is its recency. For much of the century, those in charge of corporations have barely been known, to the public as remote and inter-changeable as civil service mandarins or Third World dicta-tors. This may owe something culturally to militarism; certainly, growing regimentation of the corporation echoed the sensations of subordination and submerged individuality that many had experienced in uniform. In American indus-try, the Second World War was felt first as a challenge to its innovative and productive capacities, then in the sheer abun-dance of trained, motivated, and disciplined executive man-power that demobilisation released. Those who afterwards joined the nation's greatest retailer Sears, for instance, would have felt like they were swapping one uniform for another: its leader for almost half a century, Robert E. Wood, was a former quartermaster who revelled in the epithet 'The General'.

'The management cadre is being rationalised into mili-tary-like shape,' announced the sociologist C. Wright Mills. 'In fact, some of the very best ideas for business management have come from men of high military experience.' They came from the likes of Tom Watson Jnr, whose father had turned a company 'full of cigar-chomping guys selling coffee grinders and butcher scales' called Computing Tabulating

Recording into the punch-card and time-clock empire International Business Machines. Tom Jnr's pre-war reputation was as a wastrel; he smoked marijuana at school, barely scraped through Brown, and cordially detested the family patriarch:

> The longer I worked at IBM, the more I resented my father for the cultlike atmosphere that surrounded him. I'd look at *Business Machines*, the IBM weekly newspaper, and there would be a big picture of Dad and a banner headline announcing something really mundane like 'THOMAS J. WATSON OPENS NEW ORLEANS OFFICE'. The more successful Dad became, the more people flattered him – and he soaked it up. Everything flowed around him, he was snapping out orders, and there was always a secretary running behind him with a notebook. He would work on his editorials for *Think* magazine as though it were *Time* and he were Henry Luce and millions of people were waiting to hear what he had to say.

The experience of acting as an air-force second lieutenant, however, convinced Tom Jnr that he 'had the force of personality to get my ideas across to others', and a commanding general that he was fated to 'go back and run the IBM company'. And the scion could see that it needed running:

> If IBM had had an organisation chart at that time, there would have been a fascinating number of lines – perhaps 30 – running into his office. As a consequence, people were constantly waiting outside his door, sometimes for as long as a week, before they could see him. He saw the important ones, of course, but when I complained about people waiting in his anteroom, he said 'Oh Tom, let them wait. They're well paid'.

In *Father, Son & Co* (1990), Tom Jnr describes his careful dismantling of the personality cult within the IBM and its replacement with a 'staff-and-line structure' inspired by

General Motors and Du Pont. He bound his council of ten executives 'by persuasion, by apologies, by financial incentives, by speeches, by chatting with their wives, by thoughtfulness when they were sick, and by using every tool at my command to make that team think I was a decent guy'. He introduced the 'contention system' that allowed his buttoned-down, dark-suit, white-shirt middle managers to lead decision making. Without his formative experiences, it's unlikely Watson would have worn *Fortune's* garland as 'the greatest capitalist of all time'.

This was a genuine tide at work, for it flowed both ways, to the extent that Charles Wilson, Sloan's president at GM from 1941 then Eisenhower's Secretary of Defence from 1953, became notorious for a (usually misquoted) conflation of national and corporate aspiration: 'For years I thought what was good for our country was good for General Motors.' Wilson is the figure many have in mind in deprecating the dreariness of management in the 1950s; even at the time, as *Fortune's* C. D. Jackson observed, he seemed a cipher:

> There is a certain special stupidity and narrowness that exists in many of the more successful businessmen in this country... and Charley Wilson is a perfect example. He knows one thing, and that one thing has worked quite well for him, and because it has worked for him he thinks he knows everything else, and then you meet him and he knows so little of everything else that you begin to wonder whether in fact he knows anything at all about what he's supposed to know so much about.

Yet probably the most influential group of businessmen immediately after the war were the Whiz Kids: ten army air corps statisticians marshalled by Colonel Tex Thornton who sold themselves and their process-control prowess to Henry Ford II. Ford, by this stage, was legendary for its chaos – in one department, it's said, expenses were estimated by weighing invoices. The Whiz Kids, who included a virtuoso financial controller Ed Lundy and future company presidents Arjay Miller and Robert McNamara, changed all that. Junior sales man Lee Iacocca recalled. 'In the days before computers, these guys *were* the computers.' With his back-combed hair and rimless glasses, McNamara struck contemporaries as the technocrat supreme – 'the first incarnation of the modern professional manager', says David Halberstam. His feeling for product was minimal. The story goes that he once visited Ford's great designer Don Frey with a set of statistics, weights and costs for a new car. Frey asked eagerly: 'Do you want a soft car, a hot, sexy car, a comfortable car, a car for the young, or a car for the middle class? Whose car is it? What does it feel like?' McNamara looked blankly back: 'That's very interesting. Write down what you think is right.' About Ford's business as business, however, McNamara was possessed of total knowledge and total confidence – a confidence he also exhibited in his own tenure as Secretary of Defence during the Vietnam War then as chief of the World Bank. 'The real threat to democracy,' he said, 'comes not from overmanagement but undermanagement.'

The conformity of company man and the anonymity of corporate capitalism became a subject for social critics, like David Reisman in *The Lonely Crowd* (1950), and William Whyte in *Organisation Man* (1956). When CEOs appeared in fiction, like the protagonist of John Marquand's *Sincerely, Willis Wayde* (1955), they were elusive and emollient: 'Authority and success had made him strangely impervious, since success had smoothed all his edges, turning him into a type interchangeable with any photograph on the financial pages of the *New York Times*.' When CEOs were portrayed in movies, they were usually enmeshed in systems that had cost them their humanity or vision. In *Patterns* (1956), conniving boss

Walter Ramsay (Everett Sloane) hired bright young Fred Staples (Van Heflin) in order to marginalise then dispose of dim but loyal William Briggs (Ed Begley). In *The Man In the Gray Flannel Suit* (1956), the more benevolent Ralph Hopkins (Fredric March) took a kindly interest in speech writer Tom Rath (Gregory Peck), but admitted himself an ambivalent captive of the system he ran: 'Someone has to do the big job! This world was built by men like me! To really do a job, you have got to live it, body and soul! You people who just give half your mind to your work are riding on our backs!' Even in generally positive portraits of business, corporate hierarchies seemed to militate against the rise of the best. When Tredway Corporation's hard-driving CEO Avery Bullard died in the opening reel of *Executive Suite* (1954), his design chief Don Walling (William Holden) mourned: 'He was a great man. The greatest man I've ever known.' But Walling, while clearly the best candidate, wanted no part of boardroom bloodletting. 'I'm not going to die young at the top of the tower worrying about bond issues,' he assured his wife. 'I'm a designer, not a politician.' He intervened only to thwart a soulless Taylorist, Loren Shaw (Fredric March), in recent times Bullard's closest confidante; Bullard, Walling decides, had built a great company but 'finally lost sight of why he was building it – why he was the man he was'. Company wealth was now as identifiable as personal fortune; Joe (Tony Curtis) wooed Sugar Kane (Marilyn Monroe) in *Some Like It Hot* (1959) with the hint of corporate rather than hereditary millions:

> Joe: 'You might say we had a passion for shells. That's why we named the oil company after them.'
> Sugar: 'Shell Oil!'
> Joe: 'Please, no names, just call me Junior.'

In Britain, the situation was perhaps even more extreme.

Profiling *The Boss* (1958), Lewis and Stewart called the British
businessman 'the man nobody knows'. Business, they
sensed, was so coy as to seek the cloak of euphemism:
'Young men who do not care to admit that they are going
into business can nowadays primly say that they are going
into management.' The situation had never been worse: '"I'm
a business man, sir!" was a remark which carried a precise
and unashamed definition of personal status when uttered in
1858, and indeed in 1908. Today it is not even a remark that
is called for in big business; it might even be described as
non-U.' As Ogden Nash put it: 'England is the last home of
the aristocracy, and the art of protecting the aristocracy from
the encroachments of commerce has been raised to quite an
art/Because in America a rich butter-and-egg man is only a
rich butter-and-egg man or at most an honorary LL.D of
some hungry university, but in England he is Sir Benjamin
Buttery, Bart.'

Not surprisingly, CEOs smarted a little. US Steel's Benjamin Fairless thought there was a certain nobility in
anonymity: 'America is full of successful people you never
heard of. Men and women whom fame passed by.' Du Pont's
Crawford Greenewalt believed that 'the more effective an
executive, the more his own identity and personality blend
into the background of his organisation'. The Atlantic &
Pacific Tea Company's *bien-pensant* Ralph Burger advertised his
trust in tradition by picking the flowers for his lapel from
the founding family's greenhouse. 'You can't argue with a
hundred years of success,' he contended. And, like the
foliage in a greenhouse, America Inc was flourishing, in ver-
ifiable ways. Even in the fleeting recession of 1957, the hundred largest corporations all made profits, and would until
1964.

The controls of Sloanism, however, were steadily becoming rigidities. For all his faith in 'executive talent', Alfred

Sloan had maintained a belief in specialised technical expertise. 'I happen to be of the old school,' he explained, 'who thinks that a knowledge of the business is essential to a successful administration.' When GM had gazumped Ford, more than a third of the bosses in America's top hundred companies had come from manufacturing backgrounds. But by the time he expressed this view, it *was* an 'old school' way of thinking. Business-school degrees were increasingly standing in for experience, management accounting systems for direct acquaintance with products and markets. A typical transition was Chrysler's. GM alumnus Walter Chrysler had stamped his name on the company in the 1920s with a string of outstanding vehicles, including the DeSoto and the Plymouth. 'There is in manufacturing a creative job that only poets are supposed to know,' he said. 'Someday I'd like to show a poet how it feels to design and build a locomotive.' But after his death in August 1940, the company lost its way, failing to introduce a new model for eleven years. Finally in 1961, Chrysler sought safety in numbers, as it were, appointing as CEO Lynn Townsend, an accountant from Touche Ross recruited four years earlier. Chairman George Love, a mining man who claimed not to know what a carburettor was and to be 'too old to learn', celebrated Townsend precisely because he knew little about the automotive business:

> He is the right man because he is figure-minded. It used to be possible to control the company through personal contact. But when a company gets this big, you no longer know all the people. You can't see that so-and-so is loafing. So you need a man for whom figures live. You control the company by a knowledge of figures. Townsend can spot trouble through them.

Accounting historians H. Thomas Johnson and Robert S. Kaplan conjecture that this trend had been almost forty years in the making: 'Until the 1920s, managers invariably relied on information about the underlying processes, transactions and events that produce financial numbers. By the 1960s and 1970s, however, managers commonly relied on the financial numbers alone.' Neil Fligstein has charted the stealthy but steady change in the character of top management: between 1919 and 1979, the proportion of company presidents with finance backgrounds increased from less than a tenth to almost a third. And for managerial capitalism, this rationalist view of the corporation would come to have some ironic implications.

The concept of the conglomerate was simple and radical. A range of diverse business beneath the same organisational roof but following different economic cycles should theoretically be inured from exogenous economic shocks. Better still, a CEO should be able to optimise capital deployment by stripping surpluses from one constituent to bestow on another. The conglomerate, then, redefined expansion. Rather than growing by horizontal combination or vertical integration, this was growth by diversification: the acquisition of undertakings unrelated to previous activities, blended into the whole by common financial controls. And in this way did the conglomerate redefine the function of CEO: mere stewards no longer, they were recast as capitalists, building companies not from new products or superior services, but from other companies run by people like themselves.

The pioneer *conglomerateur* was Whiz Kid *emeritus* Tex Thornton who after falling out with Henry Ford II then Howard Hughes borrowed $1.5 million to acquire a small vacuum-tube maker, on top of which he piled another seventeen businesses. No theme or pattern united the activities of what became Litton Industries as its sales grew from $3 million to $100 million. Among its products were calculating machines, cash registers, price tags, label adhesives, office furniture, trading stamps, medical devices, marine navigation systems and warships. But it was a trend-setter. Litton's lavish annual report had the quality and gloss of an auction house catalogue. Thornton became a darling of the Great Society.

Still more successful – so successful as to be sinister – was Harold Geneen, of whom it was said that 'the g is soft, as in Jesus, not hard, as in God'. ITT, a lacklustre collection of American telephone companies with annual sales of less than $1 million when he became its CEO in 1959, acquired 275 companies in two decades, from Avis and Sheraton Hotels to Aetna Finance and Hartford Insurance. Geneen was all-seeing, all-knowing, and would have been all-doing 'if I had enough arms and legs'. As it was, he kept the managers of a workforce that grew to 350,000 in a state of exhilarated terror, presiding over 200 days of meetings a year in unflagging pursuit of the 'cold, hard facts'. It was said that he could sit for twelve hours, and was accompanied on trips by as many as fourteen briefcases; certainly he inspired scores of imitators, such as Peter Grace of W. R. Grace, so fervently of the faith that 'numbers are reality' that he pasted spreadsheets in the corridors of hotels in which he resided, and Charles Bluhdorn, whose Gulf & Western was the model for Engulf & Devour in Mel Brooks' *Silent Movie* (1976). A worshipful media, as ever, played its part. The origins of Britain's infamous Slater Walker lay in an *Evening News* series at the end of 1961 about rising young executives; among those selected in 'The Under Forties' by City editor David Malbert were Jim Slater, a go-getting thirty-two-year-old director at truck- and London bus-builders AEC, and Peter Walker, the cool finance director of Rodwell Group (later Conservative minister Lord Walker). Their combine became synonymous in Britain with relentless acquisition, ceaseless speculation and, finally, abject ruin.

For as quickly as conglomerates came into fashion so they went: groups became so diverse as to make meaningful profit targets unascertainable, competition for capital unmanageable, and accounts unintelligible. In the eighteen months to 1970 the average price of the ten biggest American conglomerates slumped 86 per cent. Seeking to explain how Litton Industries' share price had slumped from $120 to $3, the House Anti-Trust Subcommittee Investigating Conglomerates concluded that its prime capability had been turning 'flamboyant sham into an art'; its 'image of technological and organisational superiority' had owed everything to 'sophisticated accounting techniques and statistical gimmicks'. Some, however, survived: GE in the US, BAT and BTR in the UK. And the 'Go-Go Years', as they were known on Wall Street, echoed loud and long. Egged on by the emergent management consulting industry, bosses everywhere were encouraged to reconceive their businesses as portfolios: the matrix designed by Bruce Henderson of Boston Consulting Group, which divided businesses into stars, cash cows, dogs and 'question marks', became history's most ubiquitous management tool. Diversification became *de rigueur*. After all, why give money to shareholders when you could be spending it yourself? Mergers and acquisitions in the US grew from 2000 in 1965 to 6000 in 1969 as even industry giants became mini-conglomerates. The cracker kingdom Nabisco acquired a toy maker, a carpet weaver, and the world's biggest shower-curtain maker. Gulf Oil bid for the Ringling Bros and Barnum & Bailey Circuses. Legend has it that British cement manufacturer Blue Circle acquired lawn-mower maker Qualcast on the strategic principle that 'your garden is next to your house'. Australia's Dunlop 'began to go Christmas shopping throughout the year', according to its historian, acquiring dozens of ill-assorted businesses, some bought and sold within months, beneath whose weight it almost buckled. The first attempt by CEOs to modify their corporations was largely fruitless. Harvard's Michael Porter has claimed that three-quarters of diversifications at big American companies between 1950 and 1986 were unwound or sold. But it left its mark.

In explaining this collective failure of managerial capitalism, economists saw a recrudescence of the principal/agent problem, the separation of ownership and control that we first saw in *Dombey & Son*. According to agency theory, managers resist distributing cash to shareholders because cash reserves increase their autonomy, and because spending on acquisitions increases the size of their company and thus their compensation. If a company doubles in size, it hires more widget-makers, salesmen and accountants, but it doesn't hire a second CEO; the existing boss is perceived to have an additional burden, for which he deserves additional pay. Like most theories it contains both truth and a host of exceptions and qualifications: there are despotic principals and rational agents, just as there are benign owners and self-interested managers. But what's ironic is that the greatest beneficiary of the unwinding of the trend to diversification would be those who had squandered the most money: CEOs. It is from the late 1960s and early 1970s that the empirical evidence was derived supporting souped-up salaries to align the interests of principals and agents. With a few technical corrections, the graph of their value was now on an upward trend line continuing to this day.

The Rise of the
Celebrity CEO

$$$

After the Go-Go Years came the Slow-Go Years. As Sloan's *My Years With General Motors* was the canonical work of his generation, Pontiac boss John DeLorean's *On A Clear Day You Can See General Motors* (1979) became the key text of his, lampooning corporate conformity; one typical anecdote concerned GM vice-chairman Richard Terrell playing Tweedledee to chairman Richard Gerstenberg's Tweedledum:

> The dialogue would go something like this.
>
> Gerstenberg: 'Goddamnit. We cannot afford any new models next year because of the cost of this federally-mandated equipment. There is no goddamn money left for styling changes. That's the biggest problem we face.'
>
> Terrell, after about 10 minutes: 'Dick, Goddamnit, we've just got to face up to the fact that the biggest problem we face is the cost of this federally-mandated equipment. This stuff costs so much that we just don't have any money left for styling our new cars. That's our biggest problem.'
>
> Gerstenberg: 'You're Goddamn right, Dick. That's a good point.'

By now, too, it was emerging that American bosses ritually spent more time on points than products. There'd been no real revision of shopfloor practices since the 'scientific management' revolution, which unions had steadily turned to their members' advantage by imposing stark demarcations between jobs and responsibilities. On pilgrimages to Detroit beginning in the 1950s, Japanese automotive executives like Toyota's Kiichiro Toyoda and Taiichi Ohno were awed and appalled by the amount of *muda* – wasted effort, wasted value, wasted time. Because their small domestic market precluded long production runs and extreme specialisation of labour, the Japanese approached manufacturing far more frugally and fastidiously. The orient was, mark you, never so remote from the occident as it seemed. If Japanese executives sometimes appeared as indistinguishable as a platter of nori rolls, the likes of Soichiro Honda and Takeon Fujisawa of Honda, and Masaru Ibuka and Akio Morita of Sony, were businessmen of great worldliness, drawing many of their statistical process controls from teachings of American quality evangelists W. Edwards Deming and Joseph Juran. Yet this was no consolation to envious Western onlookers. On the contrary, it made Japanese advances more galling: their techniques were both extremely portable *and* culturally embedded. Fujisawa's elegant paradox was that 'Japanese and American management is 95 per cent the same and differs in all important respects.' As American businessmen scrambled to assimilate *kaizen*, *kanban* cards, PDCA cycles, and *pokayoke* devices in the 1970s, their confidence took a severe knock. Generally, the larger the industry, the less prepared it was for the *tsunami* of economic rivalry. Symbolic of what seemed topsy-turvy values was the day in July 1974 when the value of fast-food chain McDonald's passed that of US Steel. 'There is something wrong with our economy,' said Senator Lloyd Bentsen, 'when the stockmarket is long on hamburgers and short on steel.' But Japanese cars, in particular, were an idea whose time had come, suiting a world of dear oil and diminished expectations, while Detroit's Big Three were still wedded to 'a car for every purse and purpose' even as purses were tightening and purposes narrowing.

Suddenly the CEO was on the defensive. Never mind *The Stepford Wives* (1972); what about those Stepford husbands? How could one believe in bosses like those nominally directing the inert insurance giant in Joseph Heller's *Something Happened* (1974), as seen through the eyes of the novel's protagonist, junior executive Bob Slocum:

> All these twelve men are elderly now and drained by time and success of energy and ambition. Many have spent their whole lives here. They seem friendly, slow and content when I come across them in the halls (they seem dead) and are always courteous and mute when they ride with others in the public elevators. They no longer work hard. They hold meetings, make promotions, and allow their names to be used on announcements that are prepared and issued by somebody else. Nobody is sure anymore who really runs the company.

In *Corporation Man* (1971), Anthony Jay saw the modern organisation as a captive of the Macavity management system, invoking T. S. Eliot's couplet: 'You may meet him in a by-street, you may see him in the square/But when a crime's discovered, then Macavity's not there!' Harvard psychologist Abraham Zaleznik struck a chord in a famous *Harvard Business Review* essay 'Managers and Leaders: Are They Different?', his answer being not only that they were but that long-term management experience might disqualify one as a leader. Zaleznik deplored the 'new power ethic that favors collective over individual leadership, the cult of the group over that of personality'. For relief, it happened, he did not have long to wait.

Among the great corporations hardest hit by economic austerity was Chrysler, whose market share nearly halved and whose stock shed four-fifths of its value during the

1970s. No organisation was riper for regeneration, and no one better credentialled to lead it than Ford's Lee Iacocca – the first business chieftain since the days of Rockefeller and Ford whose reputation would come to rival that of his company. A skilful salesman, Iacocca's most successful promotion had been of himself in 1964, when he'd claimed credit for the sporty, spunky Mustang. Not that he'd dreamed it, designed it or even named it. His contribution to its creation was smuggling it past Ford's querulous bureaucrats, board and boss – which landed him on the covers of *Time* and *Newsweek* in the same week, and earned him the undying enmity of Henry Ford II, who finally sacked him with the tart explanation: 'I just don't like you.'

When Iacocca joined it in September 1979, Chrysler was poised to default on debts of $4.75 billion. He persuaded its 400 banks to forgive $1.1 billion in return for preferred stock, and the US government to guarantee another $1.2 billion. But Iacocca's chief triumph, as with the Mustang, was in putting a face on the company – his own. He endorsed newspaper ads – 'Would America Be Better Off Without Chrysler?' – defending the government bail-out. He appeared in the first of eighty television commercials spruiking a money-back guarantee if people disliked their new Chryslers. He identified with popular, patriotic causes, including a charity to refurbish the Statue of Liberty. *Fortune* slapped him on its cover in August 1980, peering through a clapperboard, with the headline: 'The Boss as Pitchman'. The pitch? 'I'm here. I'm real and I'm responsible for this company. And to show that I mean it, I'm signing on the dotted line.'

Chrysler's revival – based partly on productivity gains, partly on debt relief, and rather a lot on using tariff advantages to raise prices rather than reduce costs – could hardly proceed quickly enough. Iacocca seemed to follow not so much a strategy document as a script. No sooner had Chrysler returned to profitability in the second quarter in 1982 than he was pressuring aides to promote him in the press:

> As other accolades poured in, the cover of *Time* became an obsession. He spoke constantly of men he knew in the publishing world who said they could help fix it for him. *Time*, however, skeptical as to whether the Chrysler rebound would last, hesitated. When John DeLorean was arrested in a drug bust in the fall of 1982, and *Time* put him on the cover, Iacocca was enraged. 'Here I've saved this goddamn company and I can't get on the cover of *Time*,' he said, 'and that son-of-a-bitch DeLorean gets caught dealing drugs and he makes it. What the hell is wrong with these people?'

When it finally featured him in March 1983 – 'America Loves Listening to Lee' – *Time* fully made up for its earlier scepticism by specifically bruiting Iacocca's presidential ambitions. The only disincentive, it seemed, was that America's social problems were too tractable: 'Running Chrysler has been a bigger job than running the country. I could handle the national economy in six months.' The more prosaic reason was the fortune Iacocca was making, harvesting $43 million from an equity-based compensation scheme over six years, and selling seven million copies of his autobiography. 'No matter what you have, it's never enough,' he once said, and he grabbed every perquisite within reach. Irked when Chrysler had at one stage to forgo its corporate aircraft, he reclaimed the privilege in June 1985 by initiating the takeover of Gulfstream, business's biggest jetmaker. Renegade compensation consultant Graef Crystal called Iacocca the 'Babe Ruth of executive compensation' – Ruth, of course, having once justified being paid more than President Hoover because he'd had 'a better year'.

Revisionists have since depicted Iacocca as a tyrant petty in all things save pay, claiming credit for every success, blaming Japan, OPEC or the US government for every setback, and playing off potential successors to prolong his reign; before he finally yielded to Bob Eaton in January 1992, the name Iacocca was reputed to stand for 'I Am Chairman Of Chrysler Corporation Always'. But it was the manner of Iacocca's reign rather than its methods, or even its outcomes, that proved culturally formative. Though ultimately just another salaried executive, Iacocca swaggered like one of America's self-made capitalists of yore. Other bosses pushed themselves to the fore in advertising campaigns: Frank Bormann of Eastern Airlines, Victor Kiam of Remington, Frank Sellinger of Schlitz, and the chicken titan Frank Perdue ('It takes a tough man to make a tender chicken'). By opting in particular to take much of his remuneration in the form of stock, Iacocca also signed up to a popular new doctrine: 'shareholder value'.

A phrase much overused, even abused, in the years since, 'shareholder value' began as a accounting concept espoused by a professor from Northwestern University, Alfred Rappaport. In a far-reaching paper in *Harvard Business Review* – 'Selecting Strategies That Create Shareholder Value' – Rappaport scorned time-honoured accounting devices for pricing business activities based on earnings and asset backing. He promoted instead a metric based on discounted cash flow: essentially what someone should be willing to pay today in order to receive anticipated cash flow in future years, based on a company's free cash flows discounted by the weighted average of its cost of capital. 'Cash is a fact,' observed Rappaport. 'Profit is an opinion.'

At the time, such thinking was revelatory. In DCF terms, many corporations, especially those still hypertrophic from diversification binges in the 1960s and 1970s, could be seen as cheap. Takeover marauders – like Carl Icahn and Ron Perelman in the US, Britons Lord Hanson and Sir James Goldsmith, and Australians Robert Holmes a Court and Alan Bond – swooped to take advantage. Market forces helped: deregulated currencies, footloose capital, the quest at investment banks and brokers for new sources of fee income after the abolition in New York and London of fixed commissions, and a global bull market in equities which commenced in August 1982. But this was also a cultural shift, reflecting a tide of opinion in favour of deregulation, tolerant of debt, aching for change, yet with a nostalgic hankering for old-fashioned entrepreneurship. In the most famous scene in Oliver Stone's *Wall Street* (1987), the proxy fight at the annual meeting of Teldar Paper, the archetypal raider Gordon Gekko (Michael Douglas) portrays himself as incarnating a prelapsarian, anti-Sloanist golden age of American capitalism:

> Now, in the days of the free market when our country was a top industrial power, there was accountability. The Carnegies, the Mellons, the men who built this great industrial empire made sure there was, because it was their money at stake. Today, management has no stake in the company. Altogether those men sitting up there own less than three per cent of the company. You own the company and you're being royally screwed by these bureaucrats with their stock lunches, their hunting and fishing trips, their corporate jets and their golden parachutes.

Homing in on the wastefulness of agents without the economic interest of the principal, the raiders seemed to score a powerful philosophical point, especially to those with recollections of the gone-gone Go-Go Years. And even when bosses did have their money on the line, 'shareholder value' was a popular rallying cry. In the proxy fight that climaxes

Norman Jewison's film *Other People's Money* (1991), 'Jorgy' Jorgensen, octogenarian patriarch of run-down New England Cable & Wire, is pitted against wily wheeler-dealer Larry Garfield – with an unexpected twist. Jorgensen (played with rumpled integrity by Gregory Peck) pleads with shareholders to remain deaf to Garfield's inducements: 'Take a look around. Look at your neighbour. You won't kill him. That's called murder and it's illegal. Well, this too is murder. On a mass scale. Except on Wall Street, they call it "maximising shareholder value".' But 'Larry the Liquidator' (a bouncy, bug-eyed Danny De Vito) believes that the murder has already occurred; he's just claiming the insurance, and distributing it to investors: 'I'm not your *best* friend. I'm your *only* friend. I don't make anything? I'm making *you* money. And, lest we forget, that's the only reason any of you became shareholders in the first place.' And the figure who turns the result Garfield's way? New England Cable & Wire's self-serving CEO Bill Coles (a sleazy Dean Jones), who's turned over his votes because Jorgensen has denied him a golden parachute: 'Lord of the manor. House on the hill. Said he didn't want to talk about a funeral when there wasn't a corpse.'

And by this time, CEOs were fighting back. Leery of 'shareholder value' at first, they had discovered the attractions of the new market for corporate control themselves, in particular that popular variant, the leveraged buy-out (where the assets of the target company were used as collateral for extremely heavy borrowings). A CEO was the ideal leader of such a deal. 'If you get the right general,' said an executive at the buy-out giant Kohlberg Kravis Roberts, 'the colonels and lieutenants will fall in line.' Generals were welcome, in fact, because autocrats were often required. Beatrice's CEO after KKR's hostile takeover in April 1986 swore by a framed cartoon captioned: 'All those opposed, signify by saying: "I quit."' Their involvement even obtained the ideological imprimatur of corporate-finance academics like Harvard's Michael Jensen, who had been urging for many years that bosses be paid in equity, to 'align' their interests with those of investors, while their minds were concentrated by large quantities of debt, to prevent their misuse of retained earnings on acquisitions and creature comforts. So CEOs joined the Gadarene rush to privatise, restructure and refloat public companies – between 1980 and 1989 there were 2385 deals in the US worth $245 billion – and usually made a killing. Perversely, in fact, top management often benefited from its earlier inefficiency: the fat they'd marbled into their corporations could be boiled away to lighten debt. In extreme cases, business seemed to reveal a kind of abiding conspiracy against itself. In *Barbarians at the Gate* (1990), the racy account of KKR's $26.4 billion buy-out of RJR Nabisco by Bryan Burrough and John Helyar, the pivotal figure is not CEO Ross Johnson, who puts his company in play with a management buy-out, but Nabisco's John Greeniaus, who cringes when Johnson promises to make him rich. 'He's blowing up Nabisco,' Greeniaus thinks. 'I'm out of a job. My people are screwed.' He retaliates by revealing to KKR how sloppily RJR is run, in order that it might sweeten its bid:

> No you don't understand. Our charter is to run this company on a steady basis. There's really no good reason for the earnings in this group not to go up fifteen or twenty per cent. In fact, I'd get in trouble if they did. Twelve per cent is about what I'm supposed to give every quarter. The biggest problem I'll have next quarter is disposing of all the additional cash these businesses generate. The earnings are going to be too big. Christ, I've got to spend money to keep them down.

Not every buy-out ended happily ever after. Many did not. The credit crunch at the end of the 1980s precipitating a rout in the junk-bond market wiped away high rollers like

Robert Campeau's Federated Stores and Hillsborough Holdings. Australia's biggest buy-out – John Elliott's attempt to
secure control of Elders IXL for his coterie – finished in ruin
and recrimination. 'Highly leveraged transactions', as they
were euphemistically known, provoked other criticisms too:
that cash being applied to interest payments was impover-
ishing research and development; that executives who could
look no further than buying their own stock were hardly
taxing their imaginations. But, by the early 1990s, when just
about every corporation seemed to have been downsized,
rightsized or excised, CEOs had never been wealthier or,
thanks to legal ramparts erected to keep raiders at bay, cosier.
Big business had become, as the academic siren Robyn Pen-
rose exclaims in David Lodge's novel *Nice Work* (1988), a
'Brave New World where only the managing directors have
jobs' – and some CEOs seemed unusually keen to keep it that
way. *Fortune* 500 companies eliminated 3.2 million jobs in the
name of 'shareholder value' over the decade – that $1 tril-
lion in takeover debt had to be paid for somehow – and
their blood-letting was emulated round the world. Robert
Horton's austere administration at BP inspired among his
subordinates the abbreviation BOHICA: 'Bend Over Here It
Comes Again'. Europe's most admired boss Percy Barnevik,
who ran engineering giant ABB, believed that 'you can go
into any traditionally centralised corporation and cut its
headquarters staff by ninety per cent in a year'.

Fortunately, that wasn't all there was to the American
risorgimento in the 1980s. CEOs of a new entrepreneurial wave
in information technology owed nothing to debt or downsizing, and fitted no identikit, new or old. When *Time* select-
ed Apple's Steve Jobs as its Man of the Year in 1982, its
reporter found him so obnoxious that the personal computer was substituted to become 'Machine of the Year' instead.
When Jobs' compadre Larry Ellison consented to a study of

Oracle Corporation, it was entitled *The Difference Between God And Larry Ellison* (1997): the reason – prepare to be amazed – is that God doesn't think he's Larry Ellison. Their mutual nemesis, meanwhile, first featured on *Fortune*'s cover in July 1986. begoggled Bill Gates, a thirty-year-old Harvard drop-out, had just earned $350 million in the float of Microsoft. He has since been back two dozen times, while expanding his personal wealth almost 150-fold.

By the same token, beyond offering some empirical sup-port to those who regarded owners as inherently superior to mere managers, Silicon Valley had a greater economic than institutional impact. Drucker found nothing to like there: 'They're anti-bourgeois people who still want to be billion-aires and greed ruins them. I've no sympathy. They don't want to run a business, it's too like hard drudgery.' Those who tried to deduce management lessons from their doings there succeeded only in sounding slightly dotty, like John Sculley, who brought his background at Pepsico to the fore-ground at Apple. 'The clues and inspirations for business sys-tems in the future,' he announced in *Odyssey* (1987), 'are to come from new disciplines and new paradigms, from bio-logical cell theory, from Tao, from architecture, and from art.' When they didn't, he lost his job. Even Microsoft, although its market value exceeded GM's in January 1992 and did not look back, has had little influence on corporate customs; for most businesses, emulating it was scarcely an alternative. The role model instead was to be a self-styled 'lousy, grungy engineer', Jack Welch.

General Electric's top job has been described as the 'corporate equivalent of the American presidency'. Welch's predecessor Reg Jones had been his generation's favourite CEO, who spoke of 'working with the grain', and sheltering management from 'the financial community and the owners of the enterprise'. When Welch took over in April 1981, he inverted this order of precedence, running the shareholder value standard to the top of the flagpole. His demand that GE be the biggest or second-biggest competitor in its every activity entailed asset disposals worth $9 billion, acquisitions worth $18 billion, compacting a twenty-nine-tier wedding cake of managers into a simpler five-layer sponge, and the elimination of 111,000 jobs in five years. The 5000 per cent appreciation in GE's stock price over Welch's twenty-year tenure mattered for a simple reason. Its changes were not about fixing an old corporation, as Iacocca had, or building a new, as Gates was: they were crisis management without the crisis. Perhaps no businessman of the modern era has enjoyed such absolute, unquestioning esteem. Even his tart nickname 'Neutron Jack', bestowed by *Newsweek* in January 1982 for the way his policies eliminated people and preserved buildings, turned into a term of endearment; DaimlerChrysler's Jurgen Schrempp now proudly wears the handle 'Neutron Jurgen'. More or less every CEO since has sought a little of Welch's magic. 'Hopefully we can become the next General Electric,' said Tyco's Dennis Koslowski. Enron was so eager to promote Jeff Skilling as 'a younger, cooler Jack Welch' that they headhunted his GE publicist.

Time's 'Greatest Businessman of the Twentieth Century' had his share of luck. Much of GE's success could be ascribed to a structure arrived at almost inadvertently, where its old industrial businesses reposed alongside newer activities in commercial and consumer lending, leasing and insurance. With GE Industrial's triple-A credit rating underwriting GE Capital's more profitable activities, GE became a financial business trading with the risk premium of an industrial blue chip. And as for working out Welch's business philosophy... well, it's hard. 'The GE Way', admirers maintain, is inculcated at its famous Crotonville conference centre. GE's 'Work-Out' sessions in 'The Pit' – where groups of forty to a hundred employees share views on their businesses, bosses and bureaucracies – are famously vocal and vigorous. In his popular primer about GE's 'revolutionary methods', *Control Your Destiny or Someone Else Will* (2001), Noel Tichy of the University of Michigan has described them as a vestige of the frontier spirit: 'These touchy-feely, egalitarian methods may strike people from other countries as peculiarly, perhaps even laughably, American. Without question they are rooted in American culture.' Yet GE under Welch was also imperial: his flattening of its management, to borrow Anthony Sampson's words, 'replaced a republic with a monarchy'. For all GE's egalitarian get-up-and-go, for example, it tended to be a borrower of innovation: from a peak in 1985, research and development halved as a proportion of sales over twelve years, and the company only responded to the Internet in 1999 when Welch wondered why his wife was spending so much time pecking at her laptop. 'Since GE had excellent managers who were supposedly free to share ideas and opinions,' Jeff Madrick observed, 'it seems odd that the company did not undertake a major e-business program until the idea dawned on Welch himself.' And in many of its doings, Welch's GE seems to have been as 'touchy-feely' as a regiment of Gurkhas. Annual rank-and-yank performance reviews isolated and proscribed an underclass of ten per cent, who were axed if they failed to improve. 'Some think it's cruel or brutal to remove the bottom ten per cent,' Welch has stated defiantly. 'It isn't. It's just the opposite.'

Welch's autobiography *Straight From The Gut* (2001) is appropriately visceral. On the subject of acquisitions, the idea seems to make good ones (like RCA in December 1985), not bad ones (like Kidder Peabody in April 1986). On the subject of initiative, you should allow plenty of it (to the likes of NBC chief Bob Wright) except when you shouldn't (to anyone like rogue fixed-income trader Joseph

Jett, revealed in April 1994 to have confected $350 million 'profits'). Even ego is a flexible concept to Welch, cringingly modest in describing his methods ('I hate having to use the first person'), defiantly avaricious in defending his rewards ('I earned what I got... I gave it all I had'). Welch's effectively enjoins imitators not to 'do as I do', or even 'do as I say', but 'be as I am'. Want corporate performance like GE? Hire someone like Jack Welch. And pay him a bomb.

The Invisible Hand-out

$$\$\$\$$$

So how much should a CEO be paid? Such a question has been circulating since Plato told Aristotle that no one should receive more than five times the wages of the lowest-paid worker. And just as Catholic theologians in the Middle Ages were obsessed with the doctrine of 'just price' – divine justification for why one type of labour commanded greater rewards than another – businessmen have sought their own laws. J. P. Morgan decreed that the highest of his men should earn no more than twenty times as much as the humblest. But such calculations have tended to make matters more arbitrary rather than less.

Executive pay first complicated about seventy years ago when performance bonuses came into vogue. They pass without comment now, but are a curious concept: one receives a salary for doing one's job and, after some occult calculus, a bonus for doing it well, as though excellence and endeavour were not factored into preliminary estimates. They certainly puzzled their initial recipients. When a 1930 stockholder suit investigated his $1.5 million *baksheesh*, Bethlehem Steel president Eugene Grace stated confidently: 'The factor used to determine my bonus is 1.5 per cent.' A lawyer asked: '1.5 per cent of what?' Grace paused, then conceded: 'I don't know.' Nowadays, this has blossomed into the self-contradictory idea of the 'guaranteed bonus' – an innovation of compensation consultants that can only have been inspired by the Queen in *Alice in Wonderland* ('Everyone has won and all must have prizes').

Yet more curious was the concept of the golden parachute – a payment to which an executive became entitled on the termination of an employment contract, usually in the event of a change of control. These began billowing in the late 1970s, as CEOs sought soft landings amid so much takeover turbulence; they were rationalised, indeed, as discouraging incumbent management from merely warding bids off to save their own skins and disenfranchising shareholders in the process. This, of course, was not the only behaviour they rewarded. Executives lose their jobs through not being very good at least as often as in the act of disinterested self-sacrifice. As agreed payments on severance for whatever reason turned into a contractual norm, golden parachutes became not so much an incentive to fail but at least an insurance against it. Britain's leading management writer Charles Handy observed that big valedictory payouts had made ineptitude as a senior executive the shortest route to instant millionairehood. Graef Crystal thought they should be designated 'golden condoms' because 'they protect the executive and screw the shareholders'. Some golden parachutes even came equipped with golden eiderdowns to sink into, in the form of consultancy deals and retirement privileges. Paul Sticht of RJR Nabisco was said by his successor Tylee Wilson to be the company's sexual consultant: 'When I want his fucking advice I'll ask for it.'

CEO 'compensation' began its 1990s inflation, however, not because they were felt to deserve more, but because it was believed that they should be paid differently – to redress that abiding divergence of interests between those who ran and those who owned corporations. The philosophy was encapsulated in the title of one of Michael Jensen's influential contributions to *Harvard Business Review*: 'It's Not How Much You Pay, But How'. Management buy-outs were perceived as having revived the entrepreneurial spirit, but their vice was that executives often ended up with personal wealth in illiquid, undiversified lumps. A new weapon was required in the apparently unending campaign of CEO motivation.

Stock options – instruments granted by a company convertible into shares at a fixed price, thus allowing their acquisition on advantageous terms should the shares appreciate – first found favour in the US in 1950 when Harry Truman's Revenue Act gave them preferential capital gains tax treatment. They were initially treated with circumspection. IBM introduced a program in 1956, for example, but limited it to only a few executives, and Tom Watson Jnr withdrew after two years. 'We don't want to look like pigs,' agreed financial controller Al Williams. A virtue of stock options, though, was that piggishness simply burdened one's conscience. The Accounting Principles Board had solicited several learned papers from experts on their optimal costing, then when the responses proved irreconcilable arbitrarily assigned stock options a zero value. A chestnut of business is the free lunch's non-existence; here was a lunch not only free, but self-service and all-you-can-eat. Unlike a cash bonus or a parcel of free shares, both of which had to be peeled from the bottom line, the only cost of granting stock options that were then exercised and the shares sold was a slight dilution of the company's equity base. They came to enjoy tax advantages in the UK too – conferred, despite his infamous threat to 'tax the rich until the pips squeak', by Labour chancellor Dennis Healey.

Of course, stock options *do* have value. Which is why CEOs scramble after them. Which is why Jack Welch retired in December 2001 with $250 million in exercisable stock options and another $228 million in stock (aside from years of basic salary, bonuses and shares sold along the way, plus retirement perks with a capital value of $73 million). Which is why Welch used them with such abandon: by 2000, more than 30,000 GE employees held options valued at $12 billion, including Jerry Seinfeld (rewarded for a final series of his eponymous NBC comedy). Which is why Welch once jested that CEOs should never appoint academics to run their compensation committees: professors are more susceptible to envy than your average rich old man. It is also why GE is often credited with reinventing remuneration as a virtuous circle: give executives and employees access to the shareholder value they create, it is said, and they will create more. The company, what's more, doesn't pay – the market does. Presto! You've outsourced your payroll.

Of course, there's a catch; several, in fact. For one, stock-option schemes cannot distinguish between how much of a share price's fizz is the recipient's doing, and how much is simply a market's overall effervescence. A general rise in equity values is a precondition of any remuneration based on stock, but the rise should not be so swift or steep that making money becomes as easy as falling off a log. Which, we know now, is exactly what happened. In 1978, Disney CEO Cardon Walker earned $1.5 million. Twenty years later, Disney CEO Michael Eisner took home $575.6 million, mostly from options, and was one of five American CEOs splitting $1.2 billion between them.

This imprecision is exacerbated by the stock option's quirky status as the neutrino of accounting: neither weight nor mass, but effect. Those who do not charge earnings for the cost of an economic benefit are apt to begin thinking that the benefit has no cost, and distribute too much too liberally. Which, again, is what happened. Many companies began issuing options 'at-the-money' (i.e. based on the current price of ordinary securities) with an automatic 'reload' (i.e. every time options were exercised, replacements were issued), but without any mechanisms for filtering general market rises or restricting the extent of cashing out. Some Silicon Valley plans resembled huge one-ticket lotteries. In May 2000, Apple awarded Steve Jobs a package that would be worth $550 million if its stock rose five per cent a year over the next decade. Oracle responded by awarding Larry Ellison twenty million options worth $400 million, though he already owned 700 million Oracle shares. By 2002, according to the Investor Responsibility Research Centre, the average percentage of companies' shares promised as stock options had reached a record 15.7 per cent.

Options, too, are notoriously seductive. They have no downside. If the price of ordinary securities falls below the option's strike price, the option's nominal value is the only cost. But if the price of ordinary shares rises, the benefits flow in plenty. When a share-price fall is so unimportant, and a rise so remunerative, does there not exist a incitement to risk, even to recklessness? As far back as March 1997, the star Wall Street analyst Bill Gurley was pointing out: 'An aggressive stock option program has many of the same characteristics as leverage. When times are good, they are doubly good... when times turn bad, the effects of stock option compensation can be quite devastating.' Which, very obviously, is what the effects were. Remember: the objective of granting top management equity was to mitigate the principal/agent problem, to make them think like owners. Instead it conferred all ownership's rewards while inuring them to all its risks. An inspired incentive – for recipients.

And what about the principals in all this? They have been, it is to be admitted, strangely absent from our story. Since limited liability had obviated the need for eternal vigilance, shareholders had been, as it were, on a very long lunch. Capital bases were dispersed, big investors were few. Only in extreme cases did shareholders band together to exercise their collective power. In one of the most infamous examples, British pension funds called a halt to Sir Bernard Docker's misrule at BSA/Daimler in December 1956 when the excesses of his dancer wife – steam yacht and gold-plated limousine included – grew too gross to ignore. These, however, were rare enough to be exceptional. By the 1980s, the market for corporate control had changed that somewhat. Institutional investors had obtained a way to notify CEOs of their disaffection – selling; if enough shares changed hands, so did the company. By the 1990s, however, even this had become problematical: with an increasing proportion of investment capital in so-called index funds, where holdings are weighted according to the proportion a company represents of its market sector, portfolio managers faced what's been christened 'the plight of the eternal shareholder'. The question arose: if investment in many companies was more or less mandatory, could investors have a say in how these companies were run?

California Public Employees Retirement System was one of the first institutional investors to think so. After becoming boss in July 1987, Dale Hanson took careful aim at GM, by now a symbol both of American industrial pride and faded grandeur. CEO Roger Smith so resented criticism of his company's dwindling market share that he threatened to close operations in California; Smith's successor Robert Stempel was hounded to his departure in October 1992 after announcing a $4.45 billion loss. Taking advantage of the repeal of legislation that had inhibited communication between big shareholders, others followed suit. When investor insurrections in January 1993 toppled three other discredited CEOs – American Express's James Robinson III,

Westinghouse's Paul Lego, and IBM's John Akers – it seemed to presage a new era. *Fortune's* cover story 'The King Is Dead' forecast the end of 'the imperial CEO'.

The media relished being part of the spectacle. When *The Sunday Times* revealed in November 1994 that British Gas's Cedric Brown had been awarded a 75 per cent pay rise from £270,000 to £475,000, the British public had what Macaulay called 'one of its periodic fits of morality'. 'New' Labour reached for its old credentials; Tony Blair inveighed against 'the unacceptable face of privatisation' and Gordon Brown the 'excessive pay packages that are causing real offence throughout the country'. British Gas's hapless boss was pilloried by investors, harangued by trade unionists and hounded by journalists. Protestors paraded a squealing pig dubbed Cedric at British Gas's annual meeting, and a photograph of Brown in a shapeless anorak at the gate of his country pile proved one of the decade's enduring images. Big shareholders were soon making their presence felt everywhere: in March 1995, for example, the College Retirement Equities Fund purged a senescent chairman and half his board at the creaky conglomerate W. R. Grace. Small shareholders, too, began marching into annual meetings like the Munchkins advancing on Emerald City to have it out with the Wizard of Oz.

Ultimately, however, the dividends of shareholder activism have failed to match the financial and intellectual investments. In his admired *Harvard Business Review* essay 'The Promise of the Governed Corporation', John Pound boldly likened corporate governance to the 'democratic political system', proposing that big shareholders be permitted to speak directly to senior managers and the board about what they think of policies and decisions. But this, as corporate governance expert Ira Millstein has conceded, is impractical: 'Boards and certainly shareholders don't have the information to run the business. And they never will have without becoming managers themselves.' CalPERS is the biggest American fund manager, controlling funds worth $130 billion, but even it finds activism hard to justify in anything other than extreme cases, because it is expensive, its rewards accrete equally to all shareholders and its costs and risks do not: campaigning against an incumbent board, for one thing, does not position one well to also pitch for its pension-fund business. The swelling ranks of retail investors, enticed into equities in the 1990s by privatisations, demutualisations and eye-catching IPOs, are even less inclined, and less able, to agitate. Regimes of continuous disclosure have increased quantity of available data about companies, but the suspicion lingers that this has come at expense of quality – wealth of information, the economist Herbert Simon once observed, usually leads to poverty of attention.

Shareholder activism was a particularly colossal failure where share options were concerned. Their spread not only went unchecked but in some cases was actively abetted by big institutions. *The Economist* noted recently: 'It has been a fundamental tenet of shareholder capitalism for decades that there should be no dilution of equity without the prior approval of shareholders. Share options drove a coach and horses through that principle.' This failure illuminates a factor seldom acknowledged as the greatest weakness of shareholder activism: it tends to intensify when economic times are tough, when lacklustre profits are to some degree unavoidable, and to lose focus and impetus the instant the market turns, regardless of the probability that profit recovery is explained by economic factors. CEOs survived their brush with shirty shareholders in the mid-1990s for the same reason that the shortcomings of stock options were overlooked: because the market abruptly went gangbusters and there suddenly seemed ample money for everyone. It shouldn't surprise anyone to discover where much of this money ended up.

Overshoot First,
Ask Questions Later

$$$

Why do people invest? The traditional explanation is greed, fear and greed – but never underestimate fear. Alexander Pope rationalised purchasing shares at the South Sea Bubble's fullest inflation by referring to the fear of not doing so: "tis ignominious (in this Age of Hope and Golden Mountains) not to Venture'. Even once decisions are made, a streak of irrationality persists. In their delightful primer *Bulls, Bears and Dr Freud* (1965), San Francisco stockbroker Albert Haas and Stanford psychiatrist Don Jackson concluded that investment was as much personality- as purse-driven. An investor gravitates to stocks that 'it makes him feel good to own', they decided: 'Just as a flag is only a symbol for a country, so a stock merely represents shares of ownership in a company. Yet there are stock worshippers as well as flag worshippers.'

Both impulses were evident during the 1990s. When analysts were prophesying a virtually indefinite boom staked by baby-boomer billions, not to venture seemed ignominious indeed. And frankly, a good feeling was all one could have about most Internet stocks born after Netspace's nativity in August 1995, with their non-existent profits and semi-coherent strategies. Apologists for booms always stress that theirs is different – and they are partly right, for each reflects the character of its age. While the business heroes of the 1980s had positioned themselves as outside the establishment, the avatars of the 1990s boasted of building a new one, based on a kind of anti-corporate corporatism. Cuddly was in: when Netspace's Marc Andressen appeared on *Time's* cover in February 1996, his bare feet told us he wasn't just another CEO. Cosmetic was cool: Amazon's Jeff Bezos rented a garage in Bellevue simply to say that his company had been founded there, joining the lineage established by the founders of Apple and Hewlett-Packard. Garages, indeed, were integral to e-conography. From punk rock's original rehearsal studios were to be heard the strains of punk business. 'Face it,' lectured fashionable management guru Gary Hamel. 'Out there in some garage an entrepreneur is forging a bullet with your company's name on it. You've got one option: you have to shoot first.'

The dotcom entrepreneurs' anti-corporate bravado also obscured some breathtaking naiveté. In his memoir *boo hoo* (2001), Ernst Malmsten, the erstwhile CEO of fashion e-tailer boo.com, writes with high-minded horror of the idea of budgetary targets: 'Being an entrepreneur was not about making money; it was about making dreams come true.' But this was because he was more concerned with designing a corporate cocktail than with trivialities like whether his technology platform worked, let alone archaisms like determining demand: 'Market research? That was something Colgate did before it launched a new toothpaste. The internet was something you had to feel in your fingertips.' Even when boo burned $180 million and was forced to come up with a rescue plan, Malmsten's biddable dilettantes were more concerned with style than substance:

> 'Let's call it Dolphin,' Jay said.
> 'Why?'
> 'Because Dolphins are intelligent. They're also friendly

and if this is the plan that's going to save us, we need to name it after a friendly fish.'

'Dolphins are mammals,' I pointed out.

Those who understood something about the investment cycle found themselves distinctly ambivalent about their impermanent, impalpable fortunes. Mercurial hedge-fund manager James J. Cramer describes in *Confessions of a Street Addict* (2002) his foreboding after the float of thestreet.com, which imbued him with a paper fortune of $250 million:

> 'Hey, how about a loan?' said one of the half-dozen smokers outside the building.
>
> 'Slap me five, rich guy,' said another from across the street.
>
> 'Mr Dotcom,' shouted another as I walked towards the exchange.
>
> Yep 'Mr Dotcom'. Somehow I had the vision that this moment would do more to tarnish my reputation as a businessman than anything else I would ever do... I had become a quarter of a billion dollar joker, a paper million-aire with no more hope of cashing out in real dollars than if I had just won a huge game of Monopoly.

In the end, big-company CEOs would outdo almost every-one. Better a boss with stock options warmed by the general combustion than some geek feeding the flames. Silicon Valley actually proved a useful ally when the Financial Accounting Standards Board proposed charging the cost of stock options against profits in 1989 and 1993. This had some powerful advocates. 'If stock options aren't a form of compensation, what are they?' asked Warren Buffett. 'If compensation isn't an expense, what is it? And, if expenses shouldn't go into the calculation of earnings, where should they go?' But experts could always be found to emphasise the dependence of the New Economy on equity-based remuneration, with a reverent glance at Bill Gates' self-propagating fortune. 'No one points the finger at Bill Gates for being too rich,' groused Al Dunlap when his Scott Paper millions were criticised. ImClone's Sam Waksal snorted: 'Has anybody ever said to Bill Gates: "Gee you've made a lot of money on the company you built – that's really terrible"?' Capitol Hill provided further gratuitous encouragement with a well-intentioned and ill-considered 1994 law capping the deductibility of executive salaries at $1 million. This only resulted in bigger ransoms: by 2000, fully four-fifths of CEO compensation in the US came in the form of stock and bonuses.

As well as making them rich, the 1990s helped make CEOs famous. Economic historian Robert Shiller notes that a credulous media is a precondition of all bull markets: 'The history of the speculative bubble begins roughly with the advent of newspapers.' Nineteen CEOs made *Fortune's* cover in 1999, breaking records of fifteen established in 1987 and 1993 (compared to only eight in the entire 1970s). *Time* garlanded two as Men of the Year: Intel's Andy Grove in 1997, Amazon's Bezos in 1999. In one 1998 poll, seven of the ten most admired Americans were CEOs. New business media, like CNNfn, CNBC and Bloomberg Television, seemed to be willing the market higher on behalf of the eager new investment generation. Hot analysts like Henry Blodget and Jack Grubman formed a chorus like George Babbitt's Boosters Club: 'Zip Zoom Zowie and Zenith!' And it was the essence of the boom that it thrust individuals into the limelight, not only because the modern cult of celebrity demanded superstars, but because personalising a company, concept or creation was often the only way to nail it down. Numbers were drained of meaning. In 1998, AOL rose 593 per cent, Yahoo 584 per cent, Amazon 970 per cent. All were still burning money. But what were backward-looking accounts in a forward-looking world? One might as well judge a painting by the number of brushstrokes. No wonder a Burson-Marsteller survey found that 95 per cent of respondents were influenced in stock selection by the CEO's profile and reputation. At what else could one look?

The 1990s boom was somewhat unusual in that, after a time, its derangement was widely acknowledged. Dotcoms were known to be worth fractions of their stated values, telcos to have overspent on acquisitions, and the meretricious accounts of the likes of Enron regarded with suspicion. Investors could be observed exchanging knowing nods and sly confidences: 'How crazy is this market?' But a maxim of speculation is that just because it's fake doesn't mean it's not real. Investors always buy after they believe stocks overvalued, then sell after they believe them undervalued; as a banker admits in Charles Mackay's classic *Extraordinary Popular Delusions and the Madness of Crowds* (1841): 'When the rest of the world is mad, we must imitate them in some measure.'

How strange, then, that the money made by CEOs as a result of the boom was always thought entirely an outcome of merit. The manner of the wealth transfer, in fact, was its most seductive aspect. Let it be pointed out again: it was never decided that CEOs should be paid more; it was theorised, first about twenty years ago, that they should be paid differently, in such a way as to align their interests with those of shareholders. The effect, however, was to leverage their remuneration to a force even harder to predict and influence than their organisation's profitability: the share-market cycle. How on earth does a CEO 'deserve' a bull market? In hindsight, the only facet of CEO swags collected over the last decade as impressive as their size is the capacity of recipients to accept them with such straight faces. And the only surprise is that there has been no mass class action of CEOs from the 1970s: judging by current pay rates, it is clear that they were wantonly exploited.

Unreal Deals,
Conflicting Accounts

$$\$\$$$

The last stages of any bull market in equities are undergirded by what participants call the Bigger Fool Syndrome: the soothing sense that however foolish your purchase, there is somewhere a Bigger Fool who will buy you out. In 1999, Amazon shares were being held for an average seven days, compared to seven months for Microsoft, and twenty-six months for Coca-Cola. Even stranger is that those skittish punters with their casino mentality and *sauve qui peut* ethos behaved with no less wisdom, and possibly more, than larger investors. After all, among the biggest of the Bigger Fools were big corporates.

Some deals define generations. KKR's $26.4 billion buy-out of RJR Nabisco in February 1989 had climaxed what *Time* called 'The Game of Greed'; AOL's capture of *Time's* owner, Time Warner, in January 2000 likewise culminated what we might call 'Zeal for the Deal'. The merger reflected the undercurrents of the times: AOL, with sales of $5.2 billion and 12,000 employees, was capitalised at $163.2 billion; Time Warner, with sales of $26.6 billion and 67,000 employees, was valued at $83.5 billion. But what might have appeared a *folie à deux* could be sold as a *mariage de convenance* between the dishy New Economy and dowdy Old: it was, as they say in the securities market, a good 'story' deal.

AOL Time Warner was merely the biggest among a host

of such stories. Worldwide mergers, worth $2.4 trillion in
1998 and $3.4 trillion in 1999, had created compounds
once unthinkable: ExxonMobil, BP Amoco, J. P. Morgan
Chase, Pfizer Warner Lambert, Lloyds TSB, DaimlerChrysler,
Pharmacia Upjohn, PricewaterhouseCoopers, GlaxoSmith
Kline and Morgan Stanley Dean Witter Discover, along with
unearthly creations like Diageo (GrandMet and Guinness)
and Verizon (GTE and Bell Atlantic), to name but a few. But
they made sense, said merger meliorists, because they followed new rules. The majority of takeovers in the second
half of the 1990s were agreed rather than hostile, funded by
equity rather than debt, within industries rather than without, and usually founded on some commercial rationale:
excess capacity (cars), diminishing markets (aerospace and
defence contracting), declining commodity prices (oil and
minerals), rising costs of new technology (telcos and banks)
and research (pharmaceuticals).

Harsher light revealed more disturbing traits. While the
1980s market for corporate control had usually involved
seeking undervalued assets, that of the 1990s often entailed
offerors exploiting their own momentary overvaluation,
using inflated stock as collateral. No example has proven so
egregious, in fact, as AOL Time Warner: three years after
combining, it was worth a quarter of its peak valuation of
$260 billion. Many mergers were also based not on irre-
sistible advantages in alliance but on a kind of *torschlusspanik*:
'door shut panic', or the fear of being excluded. The
UBS/Swiss Bank and Citibank/Travelers mergers in
March/April 1998, for example, inspired scores of imita-
tors, with very mixed results. And as John Cassidy puts it in
his book *dot.con* (2001), many executives during the dotcom
and telco booms seemed to believe they had 'a fiduciary
responsibility to their shareholders to waste large sums on
dubious online ventures': it was viewed as 'the inevitable

and, indeed, desirable cost of moving into the twenty-first century'. Lord Simpson, for example, was cheered on as Marconi accumulated debts of £4 billion while trying to become a force in telecommunications: when its purchase of the American Internet company Fore Systems was hailed as a coup, the company's market value soared to £34.5 billion. By August 2002, however, when Marconi's lenders agreed on a recapitalisation that left shareholders with next to nothing, it was worth a paltry £50 million. Shares once worth £12 were being quoted at 3.6p.

Although a greedy and parasitic intermediation industry has evolved to enable mergers and acquisitions, too, the buying of corporate assets is always the easy part. Nobody has developed a template for what follows a merger. One of big business's dirty secrets is that few combinations fulfil expectations, even remotely. In her excellent guide, *Successful Mergers* (2002), Marion Devine contends paradoxically that as many as seven in ten fail. Dozens of studies have concluded that companies founded on mergers underperform sector peers, that bidding companies generally incur increased costs and narrowed margins after takeovers, and find headcounts stubbornly resistant to reduction. Every company embarking on a merger hopes to form part of the successful minority rather than the unsuccessful majority, yet somehow a shadow usually falls between the idea and the reality. The *fin de siècle* frenzy in mergers and acquisitions already looks problematical. A survey by KPMG Consulting released in February 2002 suggested that more than a third of the biggest cross-border acquisitions agreed at the zenith of the bull market were already being unwound. As the archetypal 1980s predator Sir James Goldsmith acknowledged: 'You cannot buy a company merely by buying its shares.'

Broad reasons are usually not far to seek. Mergers entail upheaval in existing operations, usually imperceptible to the

CEOs hatching them, the boards approving them and the investment bankers, lawyers, investigating accountants and management consultants cheering them on. Workforces are combined with the expectation that many will go. Delicate systems and networks of understanding are shivered to fragments. Managements accustomed to competing are told to cooperate. When service standards suffer, competitors target dissatisfied customers, refractory suppliers and talented staff. Intra-industry combinations run the gauntlet of anti-trust legislation. Cross-border mergers are befogged by cultural misunderstanding. Such factors are always underestimated. 'People ultimately learn to work together,' said John Reed airily after Citibank, of which he was the CEO, merged with Travelers. 'They may not like it. They may complain a lot. But in five years time they'll be surprised at how well they've learned to get on.' After nine months, he'd lost his confidence: 'I'm trying hard to understand how to make this work. I will tell you that it's not simple, it's not easy, and it's not necessarily clear to me that it will be successful.' The following month, he lost his job.

In a structural sense, bigger is always harder – thus C. Northcote Parkinson's famous maxim that 'growth brings complexity, and complexity decay'. In a financial sense, bigger is also more expensive – while everyone hopes for a bargain, sellers set their price knowing that takeovers tend to involve a concentration on the chase rather than its object. And however powerful and impressive the appearance, furthermore, a united group remains beholden to the business cycle and market conditions. When Australia's AMP stormed into the UK in the 1990s, gathering up such venerable institutions as Pearl Assurance, London Life and NPI, it was steadily broadening and deepening its exposure to an equities boom about to peak and an investment product market growing only at the most expensive (capital-guaranteed)

end. Size and scale conferred no market power; like a wind-
jammer with all its canvas aloft in a hurricane, AMP finished
its takeover spree more rather than less vulnerable to the
forces it faced.

Given this ruinous record, why would any CEO voluntar-
ily initiate a takeover? Two reasons usually suggest themselves. First, there's boredom. Takeovers are exciting: it's
more glamorous to spend billions on an acquisition than
time on improving stock turn and reducing inventory.
Second, there's vanity. Takeovers attract attention and
kudos: a droll 1995 study by Columbia University's
Matthew Hayward and Donald Hambrick confirmed statis-
tically a long-suspected link between the premiums paid
for target companies and the self-aggrandisement of CEOs,
measured by salary and media exposure. If these reasons
seem frivolous, they steer us towards a troubling third: that
it's easy. The urge to merge usually reflects pressure in a
company's core business, the fixing of which would other
wise involve both detailed understanding of its operations
and unpleasant choices. Although it's a short-term solution
to a long-term problem and reflects a poverty rather than a
wealth of executive imagination, it's usually much simpler
to acquire. Everyone's happy when a merger is consum-
mated. For the acquired, it's a big pay day. Gilded ripcords
release voluminous golden parachutes. For the acquirer,
big pay days impend. Like the generals of a junta pinning
medals on one another, everyone rewards themselves
with a pay rise and a hearty helping of options to reflect
the larger group. After the analysts' approbation, of
course, comes some hard graft: combining wary workforces, the search for savings, the elimination of duplica-
tions, the curbing of rivalries. But by the time cracks
appear, shrewd dealmakers will already have departed.
Cynics might suspect CEOs of steering companies toward

acquisitions because they know that the credit for the compelling conception will be theirs, blame for the resultant write-downs and write-offs not.

An excessively cynical formulation? While one would hope so, it is undeniable that stockmarkets are set up to privilege short-term activity over long, and that remuneration has come to reflect this. Because the value of options is enhanced by fluctuations in the value of the underlying security, in fact, the incentive is to grander designs, greater gambles. Business 2.0 recently published research by Stephen Bryan of Babcock School of Management at Wake Forest University showing that companies with high concentrations of stock options tended to have more volatile prices. 'In other words, if you're an executive with lots of stock options, it's in your interest to make decisions that increase risk and hence increase the amount by which a stock's value jumps around,' pointed out columnist Thomas Stewart. 'That incentive is strengthened because you're playing with someone else's money. Since the option costs you nothing, you're more likely to play fast and loose than you would if the money were your own and hard-earned.' As for the future, Stanford's James Collins has observed, the failure of a former employer, while regrettable, does have its reputational advantages: 'What better testament to your personal greatness than that the place falls apart after you leave?'

We have strayed far from the original idea that rewarding executives with stock would strengthen their sympatico with shareholders. On the contrary: because what gratifies investors in the short-term is not always in a company's interests long-term, it can provoke as many bad business calls as good. But there's more: as at Enron, sundry telcos and dotcoms, it may encourage dishonesty. Fully valued stock price: good. Overvalued stock price: better. Absurdly inflated share price based on sham accounts: best — at least if you're a seller.

What might be politely called the inexactitude of financial statements has been an aspect of recent corporate capers that many have found baffling. Accountants are meant to be vigilant, diligent and dull. Accounts themselves, however, have always been infinitely flexible. 'There is no true number in accounting,' said former Securities and Exchange Commission boss Harvey Pitt. 'And if there were, auditors would be the last people to find it.' Business lore is strewn with variations on the immortal exchange between Ford's Arjay Miller and his chief accountant Charles Martindale. Asked what profits would be next month, Martindale replied: 'What do you want them to be? I can make them anything you want.'

Inducements to creative accounting, of course, usually flow the other way, from chief to underling. And during the 1990s such propositions were usually heeded, because the underling already owed the chief a good deal. A 1999 CFO poll found that thirty-nine per cent of CEOs had fired their last chief financial officer, and three-quarters had personally hired the latest incumbent, mostly in the last three years. These CFOs, moreover, were not the beancounters of yore. A Spencer Stuart survey of *Fortune* 500 companies in 2002 found that only a fifth of CFOs were certified practising accountants. Quizzed about Enron's practices at the February 2002 congressional hearings following its collapse, Jeff Skilling protested: 'I am not an accountant.' And neither was his CFO Andrew Fastow, nor his deputy Michael Kopper, nor treasurer Jeff McMahon. Nor was WorldCom's CFO Scott Sullivan, nor Global Crossing's CFO Dan Cohrs: like Skilling, they either had MBAs or possessed some other non-accounting qualification. No wonder they led the trend of designing profits to fit forecasts rather than vice versa.

Earnings 'smoothing' is far from difficult. Businesses

always have alternatives in when and how to recognise a profit or a loss. In the 1990s, it became *de rigueur*: predictable earnings that met or even slightly exceeded forecasts became part of the way companies endeared themselves to investors and analysts. GE under Welch was so adept at such practices as timing asset sales to offset restructuring charges and write-downs that it missed quarterly earnings forecasts only twice in his reign, and churned out 16–18 per cent earnings growth a year like a veritable machine, as though impervious to exogenous shocks and the economic cycle. Balance sheets are even simpler, and thus more tempting, to manipulate. Because they are merely a 'snapshot' of a company's assets and liabilities on the last day of a financial year, such fictions as are perpetrated need only be temporary. Yet what became striking during the 1990s was how eagerly the manipulation of financial accounts by managements invoking 'shareholder value' was abetted by like-minded auditors. A core principle of conservative accounting, for example, is that decreases in an asset's value should be recognised at once, and increases only on sale. But accountants during the boom cheerfully fell in with 'mark-to-market' practices: immediate recognition of increases in the value of investments, usually with some effort to book in growth as revenue even where the profit was not crystallised. All sorts of practices could be justified, from the consignment of lumpy assets and their lumpier debts to special-purpose entities off the balance sheet, to treating infrastructure and marketing expenditures as investments to be written off over a number of years instead of charging them against earnings. Because, it was tacitly acknowledged, if you wouldn't sign off, someone else probably would, and dissent could be expensive. Having cultivated management consulting operations more lucrative than their accounting functions, the 'Big Five' auditors were at the time so vulnerable to having their arms twisted that they usually did it themselves – and smiled as they did so.

Respectable arguments exist for flexibility in accounting – not all businesses are the same. But when everyone is inflating their assets and elasticising their earnings, exaggeration tends to become the norm: it has been estimated that, at the height of the last boom, profits at the top 500 American companies were overstated by as much as twenty per cent. There was usually little subtlety involved. The manoeuverings were often as crude as they were large. WorldCom perpetrated the startlingly primitive ruse of classifying network maintenance costs and payments to local telephone companies as 'capital expenses', or investments, to the extent of $9 billion: unconscious obeisance to Goebbels' law of propaganda, that a single big lie is preferable to many small ones.

The most surprising aspect of the theory of getting bosses to think like owners, however, is not that it encourages dishonesty, but that it seems to encourage little else. Empirical evidence that equity-based compensation makes more conscientious bosses, rather than merely richer ones, has proved stubbornly elusive. Studies at Harvard and Wharton in the late 1990s found that compensation of both executives and directors was not predictive of profitability. James Collins reached similar conclusions in the studies that composed his bestselling *Built to Last* (1994) and *Good to Great* (2001): 'The idea that the structure of executive compensation is a key driver in corporate performance is simply not supported by the data.' Still more recent and thorough research by the husband and wife team of Catherine Daily and Dan Dalton of the Kelley School of Business at Indiana University, examining 200 companies over thirty years, found 'no relationship whatsoever' between how much of a company is owned by its executives and how it does.

This, of course, challenges all the pieties. If holding shares doesn't make feckless managers behave like responsible owners, what will? Oddly enough, however, the lack of correlation makes a certain sense. Shareholders are not collegial. Ownership is essentially a selfish business; the fortunes of other investors are not your concern. The historic evidence, indeed, is that big shareholders have concerned themselves little with smaller ones. Rockefeller, for example, declined to list Standard Oil on Wall Street: 'It was better that all our people concentrate their attention on developing the business rather than be distracted by the stockticker.' And Ford so resented minority shareholders that he tried starving them out with peppercorn payments, to the extent that the Dodge brothers had to sue him in Michigan's Supreme Court in 1917 before the Ford Motor Company would disgorge $19 million in dividends; Ford bemoaned at the trial that 'awful' success kept him from the 'fun' of reinvestment: 'We don't seem to be able to keep the profits down.' Ironically, Sloan showed more concern with the interests of shareholders than either of his great entrepreneurial forbears, though this was largely an outcome of his carping disgust with the New Deal, and his belief in equity investment as a political bulwark: 'Our goal should be to have every American a stockholder in business enterprise. Under such circumstances, the trend toward socialism might be retarded. It might even be averted.' It also cohered with his view of the company as primarily a vehicle for 'executive talent', which under conditions of more dispersed corporate ownership enjoyed freer reign, greater liberty to retain excess profits, and wider discretion to spend them.

It's arguable, in fact, that the CEOs retrofitted as owners during the 1990s failed not because they didn't act like shareholders, but because they did. Equities culture during the period stressed trading and turnover; the dotcom stampede involved the minting of millions in minutes. The practice of management became contaminated by the ethos of investing: bosses decided that in an equity-market environment where everyone looked after their own interests first, they should do the same. The stockmarket has often been likened to a casino; it became during the last decade like a casino in which the house was allowed to place bets as well. If their corporation had no purpose other than to 'create shareholder value' through a price outperforming the index, so what if, at the end of the day, it did not exist? And no wonder, under this philosophy, that it often ceased to.

Given that this situation is unlikely to change, should we forget about the valourisation of maximising shareholder value? Not necessarily. Even Allan Kennedy, whose *The End of Shareholder Value* (2000) prophesies its overthrow, admits that the creed 'can take a substantial share of the credit for the undoubted gains in productivity and performance seen in the 1990s'. Bear in mind, too, that the 1990s involved a particularly narrow interpretation of duty to shareholders: above all, pump up the share price. Were we to think of shareholder value in terms of dividends distributed, the CEOs who bankrolled their ambitions by arrogating excess profits to themselves served investors appallingly. How much better off would shareholders at AT&T, Allianz and Granada/ Carlton Communications have been if their companies had disgorged the cash they were about to fritter away on TCI/MediaOne, Dresdner Bank and ITV Digital respectively? What it might be helpful to do, however, is rethink our concept of corporations, which despite ample counterevidence remains distinctly mechanistic: a device grinding people and product into profit.

No company seeks to maximise earnings at all times. In one of his famously peppery commentaries in *Price, Cost and Output* (1958), P. J. D. Wiles suggested that this was ingrained: 'Business men do not in fact maximise their profit because they cannot do so, because they are too stupid, and because even if they were not stupid there would generally be many practical difficulties in the way.' But even if this were true, there is also a tacit understanding that a degree of waste, of duplication, of excess expense, is inherent in all commercial activity; it may even be the difference between an inviting workplace and a demoralised one, a company that can withstand exogenous shocks and one that cannot. Anecdotal evidence suggests that it's probably better to be a little inefficient than too astringent. At Marks & Spencer's, for example, the cost consciousness of old boss Simon Marks ('Good goods will sell arse upwards,' he once said) and the £1 billion profit obsession of new boss Richard Greenbury wrought a heavy toll. Though floor space was expanded almost a third between 1991 and 1998, Marks & Spencer's kept such a tight lid on headcount that finding assistance became nigh impossible. The retailer's abiding aversion to fitting rooms and toilets, and to stocking baby or XL clothes, also smacked increasingly of high-handedness. The outcome was inevitable: a sudden, precipitous collapse in sales in 1998 that almost cost the chain its independence. The most parsimonious cheese-parer among telco bosses was, *mirabile dictu*, Bernie Ebbers, who insisted on taxis rather than limousines, motels rather than hotels, and scorned corporate jets. Not long before the company hit the buffers in June 2002, Ebbers convened a meeting with senior executives that they expected would reveal a masterplan for recapitalisation:

> But instead of hearing his grand plans for WorldCom's future, the baffled executives heard their esteemed CEO go into a tirade about the theft of coffee in the company break room. Ebbers had suspected someone was nicking coffee bags, so he matched the filters and bags. At the end of the month, the filters outnumbered the bags, meaning coffee bags were indeed being stolen. Ebbers advised his executives

to make sure to count the filters and bags in their own divisions and reminded them to push up thermostats to keep
air-conditioning bills down.

The difference between efficiency and effectiveness, though,
is best illustrated by the meagre dividend of downsizing in
the late 1980s and early 1990s. Most job hackers became
repeat offenders. One celebrated survey found that two-
thirds of big payroll shrinkers had to do it a second and even
a third time: the workers went away, but the work didn't,
and those left behind were left to dwell on their diminished
sense of reciprocity. 'Think about meeting someone and
falling in love,' wrote Stanford's Jeffrey Pfeffer in contem-
plating the new corporate customs in *The Human Equation*
(1998). 'You tell the person, "I care about you and want you
to be with me. Come be with me, take care of me, be loyal
to me and devoted to my interests – and by the way, when I
find you no longer interesting or useful, you're out."'

Strangely, it is still considered a tribute to refer to a CEO
as a 'cost fanatic'. But fanaticism, as George Santayana
remarked, 'consists of redoubling your effort when you have
forgotten your aim'. Sharp increases in returns on shareholders' funds can actually be a warning: someone is stint-
ing where they haven't been; someone is running more risks
than they were. And share price spikes merely benefit a few
lucky sellers at the expense of the rest. Warren Buffett's
words, as ever, are wisest: 'We do not wish to maximise the
price at which Berkshire Hathaway shares trade.... We wish
for them to trade in a narrow range centred at their intrinsic
value.'

The view of the corporation as merely a means to the creation of shareholder value should be seen as comparable to
that much-despised fantasy figure Rational Economic
Man: a useful simplification, but a silly assumption. It's helpful
for CEOs to think of serving shareholders; what's destructive

is sacralising the shareholders' position, and doing everything legal, less legal and downright dubious in order to enrich them. This isn't because the service of shareholders encourages the pauperising of what are now popularly known as 'stakeholders' – that weird word, with its quaint echo of Dr Van Helsing. It's simply bad commercial sense: a company is no more its share price than a book is its title. The cult of shareholder value, as it has been practised recently, confuses means and ends. Companies do not exist to make profits; they make profits in order to exist. To say otherwise, Peter Drucker has observed, is to substitute legal fiction for social reality: 'The corporation is permanent, the shareholder is transitory. It might even be said without exaggeration that the corporation is really socially and politically *a priori* whereas the shareholders' position is derivative and exists only in the contemplation of law.'

Charles Handy dismisses as myth 'that it is the shareholders who run the business and that it is for them that we all work'. He champions 'existential' corporations: 'What, then, is a company for in this new, more blended, world? The only real answer, I suggest, is "for itself".' This probably pushes us too far in the opposite direction, toward unaccountability and opacity: democracy's shortcomings do not justify autocracy. But sound reasons exist for reducing shareholders to the ranks, as it were. The principle that all shareholders are alike has always been somewhat contentious. Walter Kissinger, one-time CEO of Allen Group, has aired a common complaint: 'It is ludicrous that the speculator who may be in the stock for a few hours should have the same moral claim and rights as an investor who has dedicated his whole life to the building of a company.' Despite incitements to activism, furthermore, most fund managers still behave more like passive financiers than actual owners: more than half the shares in the top 350 British companies aren't voted.

So how have their interests come to precede all others? Marjorie Kelly has argued that shareholders have become like feudal lords, contributing nothing yet expecting still the lion's share of wealth:

> The productive risk in building businesses is borne by entrepreneurs and their initial venture investors, who do contribute real investing dollars, to create real wealth. Those who buy stock at sixth- or seventh-hand, or one-thousandth hand, also take a risk – but it is a risk speculators take among themselves, trying to outwit one another, like gamblers.

The irreverent might wonder whether responsible CEOs should align their interests with such reprobates at all.

Brand Loyalty

$$$

The stockmarket wasn't the only market to which CEOs attended during the last decade; turnover in another security, thinly traded but eye-catching, was followed with special avidity: themselves. At one time, executives rose to leadership on seniority and technical skill, on their ability to perceive what was happening in their market and in their company. Decades of business-school education, the development of management information and accounting systems, and the accumulation of ideas and images about what CEOs look and sound like changed that. Innovation is important to business, but not where people are concerned: here, as C. Wright Mills observed, known quantities and familiar models are preferred:

> The fit survive and fitness means, not formal competence – there probably is no such thing for top executive positions – but conformity with the criteria of those who have succeeded. To be compatible with the top men is to act like them, to look like them, to think like them: to be of and for them – or at least to display oneself to them in such a way as to create that impression. This in fact is what is meant by 'creating' – a well-chosen word – 'a good impression'.

When all candidates for a job have similar backgrounds,

and access to similar information, other factors distinguish them. Rosabeth Moss Kantor concluded that advancement in big business boiled down to five factors: appearance, personality, aggressiveness, executive stature and promotability. She too found expertise trading at a discount. 'The interesting thing about these five essential ingredients,' she remarked, 'is that they don't include professional competence.' She conjectured that above a certain hierarchical level, competence was assumed – the emphasis fell instead on relations with peers and subordinates.

This had two implications. It became possible to reach the top, as Henry Mintzberg put it, 'without ever getting your hands on the clay of industrial experience'. The days when retail magnate J. C. Penney taught his own staff to wrap goods, and Walt Disney wandered Disneyland picking up garbage, were past. Executives could still be, say, retailers or bankers; but all, ultimately, were managers, skilled primarily in the science of management. This being so, it became an option to recruit at senior level from outside your company, your industry, even your country: if a corporation was a corporation, management and personal chemistry the key to success, the bosses to employ were outsiders with existing track records rather than insiders who might develop them. Thus, the rise of the 'brand-name CEO'. Lee Iacocca had merely moved from one leading industry participant to another; the 'brand-name CEO', like Lou Gerstner, superman of American Express, RJR Nabisco and IBM, leapt tall industries in a single bound. John Kotter's famous study of fifteen great bosses, *The General Managers* (1982), had revealed that they had spent an average of eighty per cent of their careers at one company, and ninety per cent in one industry; the new path to greatness seemed to be that of Al Dunlap, who boasted of his promiscuity: 'When things are going well, where's the challenge in that? Eventually I have gotten bored every place I have been.'

Dunlap, who rejoiced in the nickname 'Chainsaw', is worth dwelling on momentarily: for a time, no CEO enjoyed more garlands. A graduate of West Point who waged war on costs at Kimberley-Clark, Sterling Pulp and Paper and American Can, he subsequently became a management mercenary at Lily-Tulip, Diamond International, Crown Zellerbach (later Cavenham Forest Products) and Australian National Industries *inter alia*. He did not simply seek profit at all costs – he preached it, sometimes irascibly, always impatiently, styling himself as an implacable enemy of paternalism, sentimentality and discretionary expense. Swingeing austerities and sweeping redundancies were his hallmark; his management style was reminiscent of the exchange in Ring Lardner's story: 'Are you lost daddy I arsked tenderly. Shut up he explained.'

Dunlap's chief triumph was an eighteen-month tenure at Scott Paper: the company's stock price grew 225 per cent as it shed assets worth $2.4 billion and 11,000 workers preparatory to acquisition by Kimberley-Clark in December 1995. 'Did I earn that?' Dunlap asked, of his $100 million in equity spoils, earned at $165,000 a day. 'Damn right I did. I'm a superstar in my field, much like Michael Jordan in basketball and Bruce Springsteen in rock'n'roll.' He even presumed to improve on Harry Truman's dictum that if you wanted a friend, you should get a dog. 'I'm not taking any chances,' said Dunlap. 'I've got two dogs.' Truman had been talking about politics, of course; Dunlap does seem to have been referring to his life.

The formula was simple. Everything that did not absolutely have to be done wasn't. As his biographer John Byrne has explained: 'If you were the human resources chief, you slashed the training budget. If you were head of product development, you trashed the R & D expenses. If you were in manufacturing, you axed all the maintenance work. And if you were in marketing, you eliminated advertising. In short, you cut off every expense without an expeditious payback, every investment related to a company's ability to compete in the long-term.' It was unsustainable, even unconscionable, but Dunlap bonded executives by a reign of terror and a rain of money, with the expectation, which he never failed to meet, that the business would be sold at a whopping mark-up. 'The environment was so abusive, yet so fraught with the opportunity for success, that you became subverted by it,' said one. 'You got the stink of this guy on you from working with him.' And for a time, it worked like a charm – or a curse. Like Iacocca, he stared from the cover of his own bestselling autobiography, *Mean Business* (1996). On the back jacket Stetson University law professor Charles Elson stated that Dunlap had 'sparked a revolution on the American corporate scene... by demonstrating that you can entrepreneurialise the large-scale public corporation'. For a price, was the message, he would do it for you too.

The demand for 'brand-name CEOs' was fostered by the bull market: this both allowed big compensation packages larded with options, and nourished the idea that merely incremental growth was insufficient to guarantee survival. The times, according to the quotable Gary Hamel, called not for 'accountants' and 'administrators', with their 'exaggerated confidence in great execution', but for 'visionaries'. No matter that these visionaries might be unfamiliar with the industries to which they were recruited. On the contrary, newcomers were needed who would not be the captives of past practices. 'The thing that has helped me personally,' confirmed Bernie Ebbers of his experiences in the telco market, 'is that I don't understand a lot of what goes on in this industry.' As Harvard's Rakesh Khurana has pointed out, the concept of the 'brand-name CEO' is an explicit denigration of specialist know-how: the premium attaches to 'the ability to inspire and motivate employees and instil confidence in analysts and investors', while 'merely managerial tasks are discounted as pedestrian and boring, or simply ignored as irrelevant'.

That bosses believe in an external CEO market isn't surprising. Hitherto, they'd followed in predictable ruts, with only a wealthy retirement to look forward to; how much cheekier to flirt with headhunters and play hard-to-get with rivals. Yet a moment's reflection offers myriad objections. A company that decides to seek an outside CEO indicts itself, effectively conceding not only inadequate succession planning, but lack of management depth. And where this is not actually the case, incumbent executives could be forgiven for feeling slighted, if not thwarted in regard to their own ambitions. This is important: external appointments always assume that the conditions under which the new CEO previously operated can be exactly replicated, both in terms of the challenges faced, and the executive talent and resources available to meet them. Book after turgid management book in recent times has extolled the virtues of 'teams' – yet we still think of the CEO singly, a heroic Hercules on stable duty for Augeas.

The circumstances of external CEO appointment are inescapably compromised. Boards know nothing of how their new man works; they rely instead on scuttlebutt, rumour, intuition and prophecy. Typically, remarks Warren Bennis, directors 'go into a kind of collective trance, rhapsodising about "leadership" and the need for it without ever taking even the first step to define what they mean by the term'. The market's structure, with its reliance on intermediation and the need for confidentiality, makes overpayment almost inevitable. Directors aren't spending their own money: they're acting on behalf of shareholders who usually have no say in the terms of the deal. And because companies create an artificial scarcity of candidates for secrecy's sake by restricting the search to a small group, they preclude any opportunity for rival, cheaper tenders. Derek Bok has observed that 'offering one's services for unusually low rates may signal some sort of weakness and thus repel clients rather than attract them', while paying a CEO more is commonly construed as demonstrating a board's commitment to hiring the best. The greater the rewards, in fact, the better it comes to appear. On the same principle, of course, armies would simply keep pinning medals on their generals until they all looked like Napoleons.

There is also an acute irony in the undergirding assumption of the external CEO market, that the issues confronting every industry are generally the same, and that specialist knowledge can simply be picked up 'on the job'. For all the perceived need for 'visionaries', CEOs appointed from outside the corporation are likelier to rely on cookie-cutter cost-cutting initiatives, on strategies proposed by the pre-existing executive team that they are ill-equipped to challenge, or on generic solutions and expensive acquisitions mooted by fee-driven management consultants and investment bankers. 'Worldly wisdom,' Keynes observed, 'teaches that it is better for reputation to fail conventionally than to succeed unconventionally.' The rise of the 'brand-name' CEO might be thought of, in fact, as management's ultimate triumph, where the premium lies not in the creation of enterprise, but in its administration, not in anything new, but in delivering what's expected. Since corporate capital supplanted individual capital, the CEO has been strengthened at every step. For a long time, he was left alone to get on with his job. He cosseted himself with creature comforts. He was invited to expand, diversify, invest, divest, as he saw fit, as though the enterprise was his own. When he was finally criticised for having grown too distant from the legal owners of the enterprise, the shareholders, he was then enabled to take it over, through management buy-outs, or simply given large portions of it on hugely advantageous terms, through stock options. Finally, with the external CEO market, he was encouraged to treat the corporation as an opportunity off which to leverage, as a chance to build a reputation that might be parlayed into bigger personal rewards elsewhere. He has, then, never been richer, more powerful, more prominent… or less effective.

For the 'brand-name CEO' has been an acute disappointment to apologists. The most successful, Lou Gerstner, has admitted that his most important decision involved not what he did, but what he didn't: by not breaking IBM up, as many were advocating, he positioned it to offer holistic 'solutions', rather than a product here and a service there. Failures, meanwhile, have been more conspicuous, including Dunlap himself. When he accepted an offer to 'entrepreneurialise' the appliance giant Sunbeam in June 1996, the market's joy bells pealed; his arrival was likened to 'the Lakers signing Shaquille O'Neal'. Dunlap relished the attention and resolved to halve the headcount without further ado: 'I have a reputation to maintain. I don't want people to think I've lost my touch. I want big numbers.' His formula proved at first as robust as ever. Huge write-offs rinsed Sunbeam's balance sheet; huge lay-offs wrung $225 million from costs; the share price quadrupled. This time, however, no bidders appeared. When many of Dunlap's short-term cost savings proved to have long-term costs, he fell back on the crude accounting trick of loading wholesalers' shelves with product and booking the proceeds as revenue. The products did not sell, returns sent Sunbeam reeling, 'increasingly desperate measures' to disguise the impact failed, and directors led by an apostatic Charles Elson forced his resignation.

Not surprisingly, Booz Allen Hamilton's recent survey of CEO turnover concludes that external appointments are 'a high-stakes gamble'. Results of companies under their leadership, they found, were either very good or very poor, and tended to deteriorate as their tenures unfolded – early figures, of course, are often flattered by the write-offs and writedowns that usually accompany a new arrival. Booz Allen found also that external appointments would more probably be fired. 'The portrait of CEO tenure drawn from this data,' the pollsters conclude, 'appears to be that outsiders come on extremely strong, are unable to uphold their early promise, and are more likely to generate disaffection among shareholders and dismissals by boards.' This seems to vindicate the Buffettism that 'when a manager with a great reputation meets a company with a bad reputation, it is the company whose reputation stays intact'.

When market participants fixate on a certain idea, sadly, even large and repeated failure disabuses them only slowly; they are like the proverbial scientist who insists on repeating the experiment until he obtains the right result. Investors have continued to show a touching belief in the ability of their CEOs' powers of transubstantiation. Knowing his reputation as Jack Welch's offsider, shareholders greeted the arrival of GE Capital's Gary Wendt at Conseco in June 2000 with lusty salaams. Indulging his $45 million golden hello, they marked up Conseco's share price by 70 per cent. But the financial conglomerate's $8.5 billion debt didn't just disappear. Wendt quit as CEO in October 2002; Conseco went into Chapter 11 two months later in the third-largest American bankruptcy.

Faith in the power of one – fortified by several million options – is also maintained by journalists. A popular feature of modern newspaper business sections and periodicals, for example, is the survey purporting to rank CEOs by their company's profitability, or analysing their remuneration as a proportion of capitalisation or share price/dividend growth. Such surveys satisfy the hankering for ranking and rivalries – but what else? Technically, they contain the assumption that all things are equal, overlooking discrepancies between costs of capital, returns on equity and accounting standards at different companies, the varying growth prospects and expense pressures of different industries. Never mind apples and oranges; these are comparisons of apples, rocks, frogs and football boots. The surveys rely, moreover, on two related philosophical premises: that the CEO is sole author of a company's fortunes, and that annual net profit and/or share price faithfully express the exertions of the year for which the remuneration was paid. These are not simply false: they are pernicious myths.

Since Machiavelli, who observed that 'some princes flourish one day and come to grief the next without appearing to have changed in character or in any other way', management thinkers have wondered how much control leaders actually have over an institution's affairs. In his famous words:

> I am not unaware that many have held and hold the opinion that events are controlled by fortune and by God in such a way that the prudence of men cannot modify them, indeed, that men have no influence whatsoever…. Sometimes when thinking of this, I have inclined to the same opinion. Nonetheless, so as not to rule out free will, I believe that it is probably true that fortune is the arbiter of half the things we do, leaving the other half or so to be controlled by ourselves.

No one would contend that CEOs make no difference at all. The CEO who is also a founder obviously wields immense influence, even in the way he can precipitate disaster by holding on too hard too long. CEOs with the confidence of investors can also be a boon, for the responsibility to personify the company has grown weightier since 'the market' acquired the status of the ultimate arbiter of corporate fortunes. In the dotcom boom, for example, a plausible CEO made up for a host of technical and financial shortcomings: Yahoo headhunted a 'proper' businessman, Motorola's Tim Koogle, to convince investors it had outgrown its youthful high spirits; Webvan's recruitment of Andersen Consulting's George Shaheen was considered a resounding vindication of e-commerce (Webvan quickly went broke nonetheless). It should be clear by now, too, that CEOs can do enormous damage in their haste to make a mark on the corporations in their charge. When it comes to assessing their agency in subtler and more significant ways, however, our metrics for determining responsibilities and individuating entitlements run into their limits.

It is said that when Peter Salsbury was wrestling with the crisis at Marks & Spencer's in 1999 he ordered portraits of the former chairman removed from the boardroom. 'I don't like them looking down on me,' he explained disconsolately. Yet in a very real sense, the past does bear down on the modern CEO: his resources, his remuneration and even his reputation derive from a present profitability based heavily on historical decisions in which he played no part. A resources company's CEO will owe much of his pay to the choices of his predecessors, to explore in certain places, and to develop certain mines or fields. The boss of an information-technology group or electrical-goods manufacturer will benefit predominantly from brand names, patents and royalties long predating him. Even a business dependent on profit from short-term trading is the beneficiary of past efforts to build its name, capital base, credit rating and client relationships. Furthermore, projects and innovations initiated now may have no earnings or share-price impact for many years – a fact that, as Charles Hampden-Turner and Fons Trompenaar have commented, fits rather less than well with market doctrines of individual responsibility:

> Giving top executives bonuses based on these [past] accumulations is like overpaying the person who waves his fingers over the player piano on which the tunes were programmed many years earlier. In practice, it is not possible to calculate what a current CEO owes to the corporation as a community, which has learned and gathered expertise over time, and what that community owes him for his contemporary activities. All we know for certain is that lavish bonuses and handshakes transfer money from the incorporated carrier of long-term commitments to the short-term extractor of personal benefits, and we must expect the long-term viewpoint to suffer as a consequence.
>
> For if, in fact, the top manager is receiving rewards owed to the work of his predecessors, but does not acknowledge this and accepts most or all of the credit for current results, why would he bother to think of those who come after him? Let them make bold contemporary decisions as he has to earn their keep! The doctrine of individual responsibility ties each manager to shortened contemporary time spans. Proximate results are laid at your door, but distant results at another.

A CEO's choices can undoubtedly ramify for generations. Geoffrey Blainey has argued persuasively that Sir Ian McLennan's faith in geologist Lewis Weeks' recommendation that BHP explore Bass Strait for hydrocarbons contributed more to Australia's welfare than any single decision of the Whitlam government. But McLennan could scarcely have been *paid* for his decision *at the time*. And a decision only begins an implementation process. Where Bass Strait was concerned, success hinged, *inter alia*, on a sweeping seismic survey, on answering exacting challenges in pipeline and platform design, and on finding in Exxon an unusually accommodating joint venture partner to bankroll most of the exploration. Even then the field's first rig struck not oil but gas, about which BHP executives knew little, entailing a plant none had foreseen, and markets none had imagined. Investments today take an even longer route, running the gauntlet of investors, analysts, fund managers, ratings agencies and trade unions, not to mention securities, anti-trust, foreign investment and environmental regulators – then they must make a buck.

Nor should one ignore in business the phenomenon of random chance. The only reason Phillips Petroleum discovered the first hydrocarbon deposits on the North Sea's Ekofisk field in November 1969, for example, was because it had a rig in the area, the *Ocean Viking*, whose use had been prepaid; it had already been decided to discontinue the five-year search. And without that find, would BP, Shell and Texaco have continued the finds that opened up the Forties and Brent fields? Resources exploration is an extreme example of the intervention of impersonal fate, of course, but, to quote John Speden Lewis, eponymous founder of the great partnership: 'It would surely be manifestly absurd to suggest that mere luck is not a very great factor in the making of enormous fortunes.'

None of this, it will now be obvious, lends itself to easy calculation of rightful reward – for the very good reason that it was never meant to. 'In general, the greater the interdependence among various members of the organisation, the more difficult it is to measure their separate contributions,' Jeffrey Pfeffer has pointed out. 'But, of course, intense interdependence is precisely what makes it advantageous to organise people instead of depending wholly on market transactions.' Alfred Sloan perceived his pioneering GM structure as 'running itself' – so as to avoid the caprices of

lone charismatics like his predecessor Durant and rival Ford
– and efforts to change this have altered the corporation in
detail but not in substance. On the contrary, in an era when
markets have never seemed more powerful, volatile, and
dwarfing of human scale, it could be argued that, with the
partial exception of those functioning on dynastic bases,
modern industrial corporations are unamenable to one-man
control, and cannot be understood in terms of simple cause
and effect. In practical terms, as we have noted, CEOs can
know only a fraction about the various processes in train in
their corporations, and understand in detail even less. As
knowledge becomes more specialised, Isaiah Berlin once
noted, the fewer are those knowing enough to be wholly in
charge:

> One of the paradoxical consequences is therefore the
> dependence of a large number of human beings upon a
> collection of ill-coordinated experts, each of whom sooner
> or later becomes oppressed and irritated by being unable
> to step out of his box and survey the relationship of his
> particular activity to the whole. The coordinators always
> did move in the dark, but now they are aware of it. And the
> more honest and intelligent ones are rightly frightened by
> the fact that their responsibility increases in direct ratio to
> their ignorance of an ever-expanding field.

The CEO's active involvement in implementation these days is
probably more circumscribed than ever – ironically, at the
very time they have never been credited with greater powers.
'Everything is attributed to the CEO whether it's good or bad,'
complained BHP Billiton's Paul Anderson. 'It's: "The CEO did
this, the CEO did that." But in the case of BHP Billiton,
50,000 people did something and the CEO just happened to
be standing there while it all happened.' With this frustration
comes a certain fear; as Anthony Jay has suggested, the real
signs of industrial entropy cannot fail to elude them.

If you are running a giant corporation, you have plenty to do without worrying about who is minding the shop. Yet the corporation may be crumbling away beneath you, and your customers may find it out before you do. It will not be dramatic, with millions of dollars suddenly changing hands on the balance sheet; it will be myriads of tiny, imperceptible failures. The car key that jams in the lock after three days, the shop assistant who does not know what she has in stock, the service engineer who promises to call and doesn't, the sullen, unhelpful girl on the switchboard, the traveling salesman who is obviously going through the motions of selling, without any conviction – all these and hundreds like them will happen from time and time in any corporation, but if allowed to multiply they can build up almost insensibly until they are a talking point among customers and start the long slow slide down the hill. They are beyond the direct control of a top corporate executive.

Cultures and Vultures

$$\$\$\$$

We confront here some elemental questions: why do some corporations cohere while others tend towards chaos? Such ponderings are loosely grouped under the heading 'corporate culture', perhaps the most succinct definition of which is 'the way people work when they think nobody is looking'. In a bad culture, they're probably looting the stationery cabinet, forging expenses chits and downloading porn, or bickering amongst themselves like the miserable galley slaves in the Slough outpost of Wernham Hogg on television's *The Office*; in a good culture, they may be checking a consignment, streamlining a process or consulting a customer about their needs, like the perky folk of Wal-Mart, with their company songs and corny stunts. Most corporations feature a bit of both; informal homeostatic mechanisms counter one with another.

Culture is a phenomenon perceptible, as it were, only out of the corner of one's eye. It registers in routines and rituals, lore and legend. It springs sometimes from a guiding principle, such as Nordstrom's famous instruction to staff: 'Use your good judgement in all situations.' It is manifested in gestures, like the freedom HP and 3M allow for unsupervised research, acknowledging that innovation springs from curious tinkering as often as from concerted R & D, and

Merck's decision to simply give away the anti-river blindness drug mectizan when no African government could afford it, because failure to do so might have demoralised its scientists. It transcends group hugs and team-building tosh. Some companies thrive on a sense of lawlessness: the Apple ethos, Steve Jobs once rationalised, involved it being more fun to be a pirate than to join the navy. But culture is usually inculcated by a sense of shared values, common attributes, and what organisational theorists call 'fair process': open, apolitical decision making that nurtures trust and creativity.

If this sounds like common sense, that's because it is. Most writing about corporate culture is pretentious, as though the insight that people look to their jobs for more than money is somehow as significant as decrypting DNA. The title 'Director of Human Resources' still sounds eerily Orwellian, suggesting a form of personal strip mining that leaves only human craters and human tailings. Pity, really. While its study involves wrestling with ambiguities, and searching for behaviours that must by definition occur out of sight, culture matters. Just as social maladjustment is often rooted in familial dysfunction, so corporate failure usually correlates closely with cultural weakness. And where this used to be a matter of organisational rigidity and conformity preventing adaptation and innovation, dynamic fluidity and flexibility have turned out to pose their own perplexities.

Consider Enron. Technically, it crumbled because it applied its model of trading wholesale electricity and natural gas to asset classes where it did not fit and where the company lacked expertise, while sneaking more and more debt into off-balance-sheet hidey holes. But its crisis was brought on by a free-wheeling culture that assumed smart people thrown enough money could conjure markets out of nothing. Ken Lay dreamed of employing 'a superstar in every key position'; Jeffrey Skilling exalted his 'water walkers'. Enron had what

McKinsey called 'the talent mind-set' i.e. 'a deep seated belief that having better talent at all levels is how you outperform your competitors'; its consultants raved: 'Few companies will be able to achieve the excitement extravaganza that Enron has in its remarkable business transformation, but many could apply some of the principles.' But the excitement proved too much of a good thing – if it was ever good to begin with.

> The company was forever reorganising, so no one ever really knew who they were working for or what, exactly, they were supposed to be doing. The company put ever younger and less experienced people in charge of business units. The company threw ungodly amounts of money at new business concepts... and was enveloped in chaos.

There were six complete restructurings at Enron in its last eighteen months. The GE-style rank-and-yank evaluation system, whereby its performance review committee annually proscribed the weakest ten per cent of employees, was Darwinian in the extreme:

> In the middle stood representatives at Enron's Human Resources Department, who, much like game show hostesses, advanced or demoted employees according to their rankings by moving placards with their names toward the front or back of the table.... In the PRC's earliest incarnations, committee members routinely grabbed a placard from the top of the table – *'There is no way in hell this guy is a water walker!'* – and shove the card of some hapless youth down the end of the table with the rest of the losers.... Once they were weeded out, managers had to choose between people who were cool and people who might be just marginally cooler.... Committee members began running down employees they hardly knew just to save their own. Executives... sacrificed good people just to go home and get some sleep.

The result was a company, especially in new businesses like bandwidth trading, locked in mortal combat with itself. Employees clambered for personal gain and clamoured for pretentious comforts:

> There was no requirement to use a particular vendor; if you didn't want to wait for something, you could just pick up the phone and order it yourself. Anyone with a half-baked idea to launch a business could hop on a plane and fly to London. Hundreds of dealmakers made a habit of flying first-class and staying in deluxe hotels, no one seemed to care. Even junior executives didn't hesitate to hire expensive consultants; sometimes different business units hired different consultants to study the same idea. The corporate administrative types gave up trying to keep a lid on things.

Culture, it could be argued, has seldom been of greater significance. Companies have never been larger, less supervised, more complex, more dispersed, more culturally diverse, more 'virtual'. Most of our work in a given day doesn't happen because someone told us to do it; it occurs because of unspoken understandings about our role, and trust in our commitment to the common weal. For all its forbidding facade, says Harlan Cleveland, corporations today have never been closer to uncentralised systems – a development with many entailments: 'No individual can be truly "in general charge" of anything interesting or important. That means everyone involved is partly in charge. How big a part each participant plays will much depend on how responsible he or she feels for the general outcome of the collective effort.' The largest gap in the modern corporation, it has been said, is that between 'knowing' and 'doing'. The noblest intents and grandest design are as nothing when the company lacks the expertise and spirit to make them work. 'Success comes from successfully implementing strategy, not just from having one,' is Pfeffer's terse summary. 'This implementation capability derives, in large measure, from the organisation's people, how they are treated, their skills and competencies, and their efforts on behalf of the organisation.'

Where does this leave CEOs? The company's profit and price cannot be reliably ascribed to what they do on a daily basis. Their actual business decisions will stand or fall on how well they are implemented. They were once vital and visible presences in their corporations, but now, *au dessus de la mêlée*, preoccupied with the demands of investors, analysts and the media, they've never seemed more remote: so many faceless suits, screwing down costs to keep shareholders sweet and demanding unswerving loyalty even while they're being schmoozed by headhunters, as their rewards depart ever farther from the mean. Far from preserving their corporation's cultures, they might even be endangering them.

Having looked at how CEO compensation grew so great, let us consider why it remains so. The standard economic argument is that management talent trades at a premium because of competition. This makes it highly unusual as a market, in that the effect of competition is usually to drive prices down not up. In fact, as we have seen, the market is highly imperfect: closed, illiquid, and asymmetrical in its distribution of information. 'Real competition tends to undermine the privileges of closure,' Rakesh Khurana comments drily, '[but] corporate directors when they come to choose a new CEO can be some of the fiercest opponents of capitalism anywhere.' The perceived CEO shortage, he contends, is 'more social fiction than empirical reality'. The hoariest and most specious assertion by defenders of high CEO pay is the claim that we will 'lose all the good ones overseas' if we don't adopt global executive pay scales. It is reminiscent of the joke about the man observed throwing scraps of paper out the railway carriage's window who explains that this keeps elephants at bay. When told that there are no elephants in the area, he remarks: 'Yes, effective isn't it?'

The methods of determining a CEO's compensation are more imperfect still. Sifted from the candidates by a search committee and recruitment consultants, a new CEO will have his entitlements determined by reference to external benchmarks: essentially those rewards enjoyed by 'peer companies' either in the same industry or region. Such tests have two chief weaknesses. Firstly, they are easily skewed by the presence of one or two statistical outliers. Say if you're a bank president and Sandy Weill has had a hot year, or head-quartered in California and Michael Eisner is swept into your statistical sample. 'When Eisner jumps into a swimming pool of compensation data,' noted Graef Crystal, 'half the water flies out.' Secondly, nobody is ever paid the industry average. This is what is sometimes called the 'Lake Wobegone Syndrome'; like the women and children in Garrison Keillor's famous fictional enclave, CEOs are always 'above average'. This has the effect of continually ratcheting up CEO pay – a process accelerated recently by turnover in bosses' ranks.

The essence of the entitlement of CEOs to their rewards, however, is an outcome of our society's relationship with money. Money, Keith Jackson has observed, contains not only value but values: 'However fulsome the lip service a society may pay to the professions which do not directly produce wealth – teaching, nursing, fighting fires – the salaries of those engaged in these jobs reveal what the society really considers valuable.' Because we value corporations as engines of wealth creation, and respect hierarchy and rank, we reward those at least nominally in charge. We retain, too, an irreducible belief in money's motivating properties. Even were we to accept that the CEO's role in a corporation is not decisive, there would remain an argument in favour of high levels of compensation. According to the 'tournament theory' of executive remuneration delineated twenty years ago, companies pay their CEOs outsized salaries not to keep the recipient happy but to cajole those vying to succeed him. 'The CEO gets to enjoy the money,' the theory's progenitor, Ed Lazear, explained. 'But it's making everybody else work harder.' Overall compensation costs would be lowered, because competing subordinates effectively sacrificed some of their legitimate remuneration to provide the 'pot'.

Not surprisingly, 'tournament theory' has proved enduringly popular among CEOs, fond of sport and fans of competition as well as money. It even has some anecdotal correlatives: consider how the law and medicine, by sweating articled clerks and junior doctors, have traditionally used wage differentials as a stimulus. But how robust is 'tournament theory'? When Graef Crystal tested the assumption that top managers at 200 American companies were accepting a discount on their market value for the sake of a 'pot', he found that the opposite was true: there was a strong statistical correlation between the pay of the CEO and of the second-highest executive, the second with the third, and so forth. 'The pay of a CEO is not unlike a 4000-horsepower vacuum cleaner: it sucks up the pay of anyone else who gets close to the nozzle,' he concluded. 'We have to assume that giving the CEO an extra dollar of compensation has a multiplier effect; perhaps in the end that extra dollar will cost the shareholders $40 or $50 when you consider the effect it has on sucking up the pay of executives on many different management levels.' Which is the sort of finding that could surprise only an economist: common sense tells you that the usual response to the sight of others' greed is raised, not lowered, expectations.

Common sense tells you some other things too. Money

is a blunt instrument for securing adherence to goals and authority. In his irreverent study of recognition and remuneration systems *Punished by Rewards* (1995), Alfie Kohn concluded that 'rewards usually improve performance only at extremely simple – indeed, mindless – tasks, and even then they improve only quantitative performance'. Knowing what we do of CEOs' Stakhanovite work habits, why do we imagine that paying more will somehow extract from them greater effort, deeper insight, superior genius? Incentives over time, moreover, come to be seen as rights or entitlements, and to lose such effect as they have. To achieve the same impact, abundance can only be succeeded by greater abundance, with a steady diminution of returns.

For all the belief in money's motivating power, too, there seems little recognition of its power to demotivate. The exorbitant rewards of a boss they do not know, never see, and barely understand hardly stirs a middle manager or worker to greater effort. The disruptive effect of big rewards was first systematically observed in the late 1930s by Joseph Scanlon, an accountant and union official at La Pointe Steel in Pennsylvania, who staved off bankruptcy with a pioneering experiment in compensation restructuring: he noted that where bonuses were paid to a group of workers, that group was likelier to support and respect higher performers, but where bonuses were targeted to outstanding individuals, the result was enmity, disunity and sometimes outright sedition. One can only speculate on the corrosive impact of buoyant CEO salaries, especially in a period of profit stagnation, not to mention the trend to gross executive payouts on resignation, retirement and even retrenchment when all jobs are threatened. Some have criticised modern CEOs for being too obsessed with appearances; on the contrary, they may care too little. Ken Iverson of Nucor, the last American steelmaker worth the name, has pointed out what seems to have eluded so many others of his rank and generation:

> The people at the top of the corporate hierarchy grant themselves privilege after privilege, flaunt those privileges before the men and women who do the real work, then wonder why employees are unmoved by management's invocations to cut costs and boost profitability.... When I think of the millions of dollars spent by people at the top of the management hierarchy on efforts to motivate people who are continually put down by that hierarchy, I can only shake my head in wonder.

Big salaries, then, are not merely hard to justify; they may be compromising the companies that pay them. And if CEOs are incapable of perceiving this, others will have to help them.

Man Over Board

$$$

Given that the coercive powers not only of shareholders but also of regulators and auditors are necessarily limited, corporate governance reform has tended to concentrate on boardrooms: several new codes of conduct for directors have recently been passed by stock exchanges, and there have been four reviews of board behaviour in the City during the last decade. In the ideal board meeting, none are silent and all are heard. The CEO provides initiative, the directors wisdom. But this ideal is elusive. Boards succumb easily to what psychologist Jerry Harvey has called the Abilene Paradox: groups agree to decisions that the individuals inwardly acknowledge are silly because they know they can sidestep responsibility. A certain politesse pertains, as Warren Buffett has described it: 'When the compensation committee – armed, as always, with support from a high-paid consultant – reports on a megagrant of options to the CEO, it would be like belching at the dinner table for a director to suggest that the committee reconsider.' At worst, a scene unfolds like the perfunctory board meetings in Anthony Trollope's *The Way We Live Now* (1875), where the railway magnate *manqué* Augustus Melmotte quashes dissent in terms echoed by generations of executive egotists:

> Unanimity is everything in the direction of such an undertaking as this. With unanimity we can do – everything.... Without unanimity we can do – nothing. Unanimity should be printed everywhere about a Board-room.... If you and I quarrel in the Board-room, there is no knowing the amount of evil we may do to every individual shareholder in the Company.

Solutions abound to this tension between the quest for accord and the scope for disagreement. The US and UK tend to unitary boards, but American companies usually combine the roles of chairman and CEO and have more independent directors, where British companies separate the roles of chairman and CEO and have fewer independent directors. In Germany, by contrast, governance has been split between the *vorstand* (management board) and *aufsichtsrat* (supervisory board, usually composed of the CEO, and various stakeholder representatives) since the 1870 law introducing free incorporation for joint-stock companies. All these models have their advantages – and their shortcomings. The American system has encouraged the collection of 'trophy directors', kept largely for display. 'Wine 'em, dine 'em and screw 'em' was Henry Ford II's immortal advice. British non-executive directors, meanwhile, have more often held office out of custom, thanks to vestigial family connections. Jonathan Guinness recently revealed his family's incuriosity about the corporation bearing their name even as CEO Ernest Saunders was enmeshed in what a judge would later call 'dishonesty on a massive scale' during its Distillers takeover. 'It was always easiest to do nothing,' he confessed. 'So I kept my head down.' Co-director Finn Guinness confided meekly in his brother: 'We may not do much good but at least we don't do much harm.' The German separation of powers has often been celebrated as the ideal, but tends to check as well as balance, and a supervisory board can be a handicap when speed and secrecy are of the essence. The difficulty of recruiting competent boards, paltry fees and the threat of legal hostilities are complained of almost universally The same current and retired CEOs turn up again and again, leavened by the occasional woman and academic, with scarcity of candidates exacerbated by the fact that those most knowledgeable must often be disqualified because of perceived conflicts of interest. The result is that directors tend to be chosen not because of prior experience of the relevant industry, but because of prior experience as directors – when Marks & Spencer's shambled into crisis in 1998, for example, there was not a single non-executive board member with retail background. Their loyalty, accordingly, becomes primarily to the CEO and to their board peers, rather than to the corporation, shareholders or employees.

We referred earlier to that troubling gulf that faces CEOs between the general knowledge at the top of organisations, and the specialist knowledge within operations and finance. For non-executives directors, expected to gain a working understanding of their companies' myriad activities in perhaps three to five weeks' work a year, often without a significant exposure to the specific industry or deep background in the enterprise, the gulf grows chasmic. Katherine Schipper of University of Chicago argued recently that a significant contributing factor to American corporate malfeasance was the 'severe lack' of accounting expertise among directors, who relied instead on 'gut instinct, oral tradition, managerial manipulation and casual conversation'. In their *Back to the Drawing Board* (2003), Colin Carter of Boston Consulting Group and Jay Lorsch of Harvard have even argued that, in general, the job of being a public company director is 'not do-able':

> Boards are a conundrum. Take a group of part-time directors and present them with an extremely difficult job, but

give them very limited time together. And then charge
this institution with ultimate responsibility for ensuring
that the nation's most important economic assets are
well-managed. How can such an unlikely arrangement
work?

One-eyed CEOs flourish easily in such kingdoms of the
blind. They have the best view of the corporation's doings,
the fullest market intelligence, have been appointed by at
least some of the directors, and have probably been involved
at some level in the appointment of others. Directors remain
dependent on the information management provides, and
often on the CEO for their continued tenure.

Discouragingly, no standard format exists for a successful
board. In times of corporate puritanism, the cry is routinely
raised for more independent directors. But while it is true
that most scandals originate in management prodigalities,
the structure of a board seems unrelated to its vigilance as a
watchdog. Enron had a board that by some lights was close
to ideal: only two executive directors, and an audit committee chaired by a distinguished professor of accounting, Stanford's Robert Jaedicke. Close supervision, meanwhile, is a
fine thing. Sam Chisholm, the bare-knuckled boss Rupert
Murdoch introduced to sort out BSkyB, has rightly remarked
that 'there never was a company that went under because it
had a board that was too strong'. But a board should aspire
to more than preventing a company's collapse: meddlesome
directors scotching every initiative are as destructive as the
dozy and neglectful.

A new trend in the US is the meeting of the board in
'executive session'; that is, without the executives present.
Jack Welch used to thumb his nose at such namby-pam-
biness, claiming that the day it happened at GE was the
day he would quit, but an increasing number of American corporations are favouring 'lead directors' to convene

board meetings from which the CEO and his circle are barred, in the hope that greater candour and collegiality will be the outcome. Again, though, experiences have been mixed. Dennis Kozlowski, who espoused a deep interest in corporate governance best practice, was the only non-independent member of Tyco's board, and let a 'lead director' run board meetings and executive sessions. It did little to circumscribe his influence, and nothing to curb the inflation of his pay.

Gary Pemberton, former CEO of Brambles, chairman of Qantas and an arch enemy of prescriptive solutions to corporate governance concerns, has a wry view: 'The only way to get good corporate governance is to have good corporate governors.' If this be so, the short supply of wise governors should be our very first concern. And, oddly enough, an obvious source of amply qualified directors, with undoubted loyalty and immense operational expertise, has been entirely overlooked. Given the modern obsession with selecting directors by their CVs, the recruitment of directors from among a company's former middle managers will sound heterodox to say the least. While the image of the CEO and top executive has been evolving for more than a century, the middle manager remains a Pooteresque caricature. Downsizing in the 1980s and 1990s annihilated hundreds of thousands; it remains the case that the quickest way for a CEO to obtain an ovation is to propose eliminating a layer of managers, as though dusting a mantelpiece or scraping off a coating of rust. Yet, as even Lou Gerstner acknowledges, bureaucrats hold companies together:

> The truth is that no large enterprise can work without bureaucracy. Bureaucrats... provide coordination among disparate line organisations; establish and enforce corporatewide strategies that allow the enterprise to avoid duplication, confusion and conflict; and provide highly

specialised skills that cannot be duplicated because of cost
or simply the shortage of available resources.

Under pressure, most CEOs will admit something similar:
that middle managers are custodians of corporate culture
and keepers of corporate memory. Actually, they're more.
They understand processes, and the impact of policies. They
deal daily with abrasive personalities, and have eyeballed
competitors. There will be reasons, of course, they have not
risen to top management. They probably lacked ambition.
They may have had limited horizons. Yet what a source of
knowhow for other directors to consult. And training operations personnel to evaluate board issues is surely no more
difficult – and probably less – than schooling professional
directors in operations. The likeliest objection – that
middle managers are inherently suspicious of innovation
and lack imagination – assumes that both are entirely neg-
ative qualities: more suspicion and less imagination would
have saved billions at telcos and dotcoms, have thwarted a
host of ill-considered acquisitions, and redirected innu-
merable ill-conceived austerity drives.

It will, of course, probably never happen. Directors are
wedded to the recruitment of people like themselves.
Which is a pity, for this seems all the more reason to promote from within. The archetypal middle manager has
always put the corporation's interests before his or her own.
They understand that their companies are more than 'shareholder value' devices. They appreciate the long haul because
they've been part of it. They also know how disaffecting it is
for staff to look up at a CEO on a multi-million dollar salary.
If we genuinely wish to curb overmighty, overrated, overpaid CEOs, there could be no better counterweight than
those who've been none of these things while lending their
enterprises unstinting service. But maybe, of course, for all
our bluster, we don't.

Better Company

$$$

Dear Business Leader...

Form letters abound in their variety, but this salutation on one I recently received from *Harvard Business Review*, the journal seen in all the best executive briefcases, immediately lent it novelty.

Your career isn't just about money, is it?

That's for sure.

I didn't think so. It's about something deeper.

Tell me more...

Something so central to your core, to what makes you tick, that you can't imagine living without it.

I'm ready. Hit me with it.

It's about leadership. Having your say. Making things happen. Putting your stamp on the future.

Is that right? The point of this sycophancy was swiftly revealed. If I completed the enclosed form and committed my credit card to a monthly ravaging, I'd be privy to the latest wisdom on questions like '*The essential skill of managing oneself*' – which I rather liked, imagining issuing my own orders, refusing them, then firing myself. But was I up to the responsibility anyway?

To be a successful leader, you have to be smart, tough, determined and visionary.

Phew.

Sure, but stop there, and you're an also ran.

Eh? Did HBR mean that these qualities were not enough? Where did that leave those of us who were slow, meek, dilatory and introspective? All was revealed in the accompanying pamphlet: '*You and Harvard Business Review*'. The combination, it seemed, was electric. The outcome was a CEO cut from the cloth of *Atlas Shrugged's* John Galt: *Leader. Strategist. Mentor. Architect. Builder. Coordinator. Champion.*

As a mnemonic, LSMABCC had little to recommend it. But as a formulation, it was both compelling and menacing, like the product of a religious ecstacy or a personality cult; one would not have been surprised to see it in the context of a tract about David Koresh, or at a parade honouring Kim Jong Il. And therein, I suspected, a source of our present discontents. As noted earlier, our disillusionment with CEOs springs from a prior faith. And a faith bespeaks a need among its adherents. For all our desire to chasten and chastise CEOs, we still want to believe. 'It would be a travesty,' Warren Buffett warned last year, 'if the bloated pay of recent years became the baseline for future compensation.' Yet part of us – the anxious part that frets about relative performance and the size of the nest egg we hope the equity market will hatch for us – still feels it a price worth paying, in other than egregious cases. Still popular, for instance, is the mealymouthed sentiment that we will happily pay 'world-class rewards' for 'world-class performance' – as though this is somehow readily and obviously achievable in the simple preference for one strategy over another. This is nonsensical, but the cult of the CEO springs from the same ability to ignore logic as Dr Johnson saw in disputation about the existence of ghosts: 'All argument is against it; but all belief for it.' It is a belief, moreover, piled on other beliefs. The making of the modern CEO has been a story of more: more prominence, more plaudits, more ownership, more money, more demands, more expectations, and above all more illusions. More, as so often, has brought less – and as Peter Drucker observed a full fifty-eight years ago, was always likely to: 'No institution can possibly survive if it needs geniuses or supermen to manage it. It must be organised in such a way as to be able to get along under a leadership composed of average human beings.' And if we think we need supermen to run our businesses, then the solution is not to seek supermen but to rethink business. Paul Samuelson memorably described capitalism as 'an effective but unloveable system with no mystique to protect it'; right now it should take some steps to protect itself.

Some shifts are already underway. The expensing of stock options, bravely undertaken by Microsoft in 2003, cannot come quickly enough. This will consolidate the trend to the use of restricted stock that CEOs must hold for the long-term, sometimes until retirement. Greater indexing of equity rewards is also probably inevitable, especially if 2003's recovery in stock prices proves a false dawn: as Alfred Rappaport once said, CEOs always wish to be paid for absolute performance in bull markets, relative performance in bear markets. Expect more companies to resist the windfall severance payments hitherto granted unblinkingly. These gratuities have long been not only obscene but illogical; as we have seen, executive decisions do not bear fruit contemporaneously. Observers of trends in executive pay are beginning also to look past those taking to those giving. The rejection of Jean-Pierre Garnier's pay package late in 2003 was one thing; more significant in the long run might be the departures soon after of two members of the committee, former Marconi chairman Sir Roger Hurn and American-born Paul Allaire, who had signed off on it. Likewise did Daimler-Chrysler's Jurgen Schremp and former UN ambassador Carl

McCall follow Richard Grasso out the door at the New York Stock Exchange. 'If members of compensation committees were more regularly held to account for the contracts which they approve,' noted *The Economist* in October 2003, 'it seems likely that fewer of those contracts would be offensive to employees, shareholders and the general public.'

Legislation and regulation have a part to play too. A variety of proposals have been either accepted or aired, those in the US being of paramount significance, representing as they do the price of entry to the world's richest capital markets; anything that provokes investors to show more interest in their investments, such as initiatives in the US and UK to enfranchise shareholders at annual meetings, is to be encouraged. Yet many mooted changes to the law appear less likely to restrain CEOs, for the simple reason that legalities are not the same as ethics — and ethics in boardrooms can be bent without breaking. 'There are things that happen when you join a company that cause you to believe that the values in one's outside life aren't relevant anymore on the inside,' Jeffrey Pfeffer told *Fast Company* last year. 'You say: "The rules are different. Life is complex." So what has been going on recently really has more to do with an unsurpassed ability on the part of senior corporate leaders to justify anything.' Business in recent times has not, however, simply fallen among thieves. Corporate depredation has less impact on market cycles than market cycles on corporate depredation; thus John Kenneth Galbraith's famous theory of 'the bezzle':

> At any given time, there exists an inventory of undiscovered embezzlement. This inventory — it should, perhaps, be called 'the bezzle' — amounts at any moment to many millions of dollars.... In good times people are relaxed, trusting and money is plentiful. But even though money is plentiful, there are always many people who need more...

under these circumstances, the rate of embezzlement grows, the rate of discovery falls off, and 'the bezzle' increases rapidly. In depression all this is reversed. Money is watched with a narrow suspicious eye. The man who handles it is assumed to be dishonest until he proves himself otherwise.

Accumulating evidence of recent corporate corruption, then, has been received with rather too much relish, tending as it does to absolve everyone else. We forget that a lot of what CEOs extracted was in full view. We overlook how naively we bought the myth of their individual genius. We ignore our complicity in the 'irrational exuberance' that made them rich. If we wish to avoid repeating this age's errors, we will need, above all, a more reasoned and realistic understanding of how businesses work, where value is added, where it is dissipated, what the CEO can do, what he assuredly cannot. We'll need to distinguish between activity and progress, between ostensible expansion and sustainable growth, between the quantity of a profit and its quality. And we'll have to abandon our fixation on the boss of the enterprise, a phenomenon whose only beneficiaries have been a small and self-interested elite who would be just as effectual, just as motivated, and wise, and virtuous were they paid a fraction of their current rewards. Casting a big star may make a bad movie more watchable, but won't make it good. In the same way, the recruitment of a 'brand-name CEO' at a mediocre corporation is likely only to make for a marginally more interesting version of failure. The modern industrial corporation was devised in order that commercial enterprise should outlive individuals, and aggregate the talents of many: trying to turn it back into 'the lengthened shadow of one man', to use Emerson's lovely line, was probably always foredoomed. Big companies are creatures of their cultures. What enables one to outperform another is far more mysterious than is generally assumed, and for the most part obscured from the outside world.

As for CEOs, their own interests would be served by a more modest appraisal of their abilities and powers. In some respects, it's very easy to be a CEO, precisely because corporations have been structured so as not to depend on individual genius. Ironically, this is not because it is an environment of impersonal control, but because it is a sum of human strivings. People adjust. People cope. People get by. A student of corporate collapses learns to marvel not only at the scale of human folly, but at the power of human resilience. All that we know of Enron confirms yet again that big businesses can cheat death for years, even decades, under management that would bankrupt an off-licence in a week. With this, however, comes the entailment that the corporation is very difficult to change; as its scale and complexity has increased, it has in fact grown less flexible and less responsive to control from the top. People resist. People ignore. Should it come to that, people quit. This is all the more reason why CEOs should be worried about how they look, not merely to investors, to regulators and to media, but to their own employees and the public, and all the more reason why they should exercise resolve, restraint, and a sense of proportion. While scepticism is integral to a healthy corporate culture, cynicism is its greatest enemy – and for this the only remedies are honesty and humility.

A Guide to Sources

$$$

'So a prudent man will always follow in the footsteps of great men and imitate those who have been outstanding. If his own prowess fails in comparison with theirs, at least it has an air of greatness about it.' Thus Niccolò Machiavelli in *The Prince* — and on the desire for that air have publishers built a vast industry. Before the Second World War, Peter Drucker has recalled, 'all the books on management did not fill a modest shelf'. Then someone realised there was a buck in it, and today perhaps no shelves in your local bookshop support so much dross. In an interview in March 1997, the veteran organisational scholar Richard Pascale recalled a recent meeting to discuss a book with a publishing company. All was well until the editor enquired: 'But can you put your argument in one sentence?' When Pascale replied that, at a pinch, he might squeeze it into four, he was told to rethink the idea.

So be selective. Books quoted in this essay are the small tip of a vast and slow-moving glacier. Drucker's *The Concept of the Corporation* (John Day, 1946) and *The Age of Discontinuity* (William Heinemann, 1969) have resisted countless efforts to improve upon them. Henry Mintzberg's *The Nature of Managerial Work* (Harper & Row, 1973) and *Mintzberg on Management* (The Free Press, 1989) are personal favourites. Also quoted are: Albert, Michel, *Capitalism Against Capitalism* (Whurr Publishers, 1993); Bennis, Warren and Burt Nanus, *Leaders: The Strategies For Taking Charge* (Harper & Row, 1986); Burnham, James, *The Managerial Revolution: What Is Happening in the World* (Indiana University Press, 1940); Carter, Colin and Jay Lorsch, *Back to the Drawing Board* (Harvard Business School Press, 2003); Cleveland, Harlan, *Nobody in Charge* (Warren Bennis Books, 2002); Collins, Jim and Jerry Porras, *Built to Last* (Random House, 1994); Collins, Jim, *Good to Great* (Random House, 2001); Crystal, Graef, *In Search of Excess: The Overcompensation* of American Executives (W. W. Norton, 1991); Devine, Marion, Successful Mergers (The Economist in association with Profile Books, 2002); Flanagan, William, Dirty Rotten CEOs (Five Mile Press, 2003); Follet, Mary Parker (editor Pauline Graham), Prophet of Management: A Celebration of Writings from the 1920s (Harvard Business School Press, 1995); Garten, Jeffrey, The Mind of the CEO (Penguin, 2001); Hamel, Gary, Leading the Revolution (Harvard Business School, 2000); Hampden-Turner, Charles and Fons Trompenaar, The Seven Cultures of Capitalism (Doubleday, 1993); Handy, Charles, The Empty Raincoat (Hutchinson, 1994); Harvey, Jerry, The Abilene Paradox and Other Meditations on Management (Wiley, 1996); Huffington, Arianna, Pigs at the Trough: How Political Corruption and Corporate Greed Are Destroying America (Random House, 2003); Jay, Anthony, Corporation Man (Pocket Books, 1971); Johnson, H. Thomas and Robert S. Kaplan, Relevance Lost: The Rise and Fall of Management Accounting (Harvard Business School Press, 1987); Kanter, Rosabeth Moss, Men and Women of the Corporation (Basic Books, 1977); Kay, John, The Foundations of Corporate Success (Oxford University Press, 1993); Kelly, Marjorie, The Divine Right of Capital: Dethroning the Corporate Aristocracy (Berrett-Koehler Publishers, 2001); Kennedy, Allan, The End of Shareholder Value (Orion, 2000); Kennedy, Carol, The Next Big Thing (Random House, 2000); Khurana, Rakesh, Searching for a Corporate Saviour (Princeton University Press, 2002); Kotter, John, The General Managers (Harvard Business School Press, 1982); Krames, Jeffrey, The Rumsfeld Way: Leadership Secrets of a Battle-Hardened Maverick (McGraw-Hill, 2001); Lammiman, Jean and Michael Syrett, Entering Tiger Country: How Ideas Are Shaped in Organisations (Roffey Park Management Institute, 2000); Lesieur, Frederick (editor), The Scanlon Plan: A Frontier in Labor-Management Cooperation (MIT, 1958); Lewis, Roy and Rosemary Stewart, The Boss: The Life and Times of the British Business Man (Phoenix House, 1958); McNamara, Robert, The Essence of Security (Harper & Row, 1964); Michaels, Ed, Helen Handfield-Jones and Beth Axelrod, The War for Talent (Harvard Business School Press, 2001); Mills, C. Wright, White Collar (Oxford University Press, 1953) and The Power Elite (Oxford University Press, 1956); Pascale, Richard and Anthony Athos, The Art of Japanese Management (Simon & Schuster, 1981); Pfeffer, Jeffrey, The Human Equation (Harvard Business School Press, 1998); Riesman, David, The Lonely Crowd: A Study of the Changing American Character (Doubleday, 1950); Sampson, Anthony, Company Man: The Rise and Fall of Corporate Life (HarperCollins, 1995); Seifter, Harvey with Peter Economy and J. Richard Hackman, Leadership Ensemble (Henry Holt, 2001); Whyte, William, Organisation Man (Simon & Schuster, 1956).

A Guide to Sources

History and Biography

The outstanding scholar of the evolution of the modern industrial corporation is the Harvard economic historian Alfred Chandler, especially his The Visible Hand: The Managerial Revolution in American Business (Harvard University Press, 1977), Pierre S. du Pont and the Making of the Modern Corporation (Harper & Row, 1971) and Scale and Scope: The Dynamics of Industrial Capitalism (Harvard University Press, 1990). A complementary study of English malaise is Martin Wiener's English Culture and the Decline of the Industrial Spirit 1850–1980 (Cambridge University Press, 1981). A range of journalistic and historical accounts of individual corporations and industries has also been drawn on: Anders, George, Merchants of Debt: KKR and the Mortgaging of American Business (Jonathan Cape, 1992); Bevan, Judith, The Rise and Fall of Marks & Spencer (Profile, 2000); Brooks, John, The Go-Go Years: The Drama and Crushing Finale of Wall Street's Bullish 1960s (Allworth Press, 1998); Gordon, John Steele, The Great Game: The Emergence of Wall Street as a World Power 1653–2000 (Touchstone, 2000); Halberstam, David, The Reckoning (Avon, 1986); Katz, Donald, The Big Store (Penguin, 1987); Kaplan, David, The Silicon Boys (Allen & Unwin, 1999); Lawson, Thomas, Frenzied Finance (Ridgway-Thayer, 1906); Levin, Doron, Behind The Wheel at Chrysler (Harcourt, 1995); McCraw, Thomas, American Business 1920-2000 (Harlan Davidson, 2000); Micklethwait, John and Adrian Wooldridge, The Company: A Short History of a Revolutionary Idea (Modern Library Chronicles, 2003); Sampson, Anthony, The Sovereign State (Hodder & Stoughton, 1973); Tarbell, Ida, The History of the Standard Oil Company (Peter Smith, 1950); Turner, Marcia Layton, Kmart's 10 Deadly Sins (John Wiley, 2003); Walsh, William I., The Rise and Decline of the Great Atlantic & Pacific Tea Company (Lyle Stuart Inc., 1986); Westfield, Mark, HIH: The Inside Story of Australia's Biggest Corporate Collapse (Wiley, 2003); Wilson, Mike, The Difference Between God and Larry Ellison (William Morrow, 1997).

Because businessmen seem to write, produce or generate far more books than they read, this essay has also been able to survey a broad spectrum of autobiographies and biographies. The following books by businessmen – or at least, as seems the modern fashion, bearing their names – are quoted herein: Dunlap, Al (with Bob Andelman), Mean Business (HarperBusiness, 1996); Eisner, Michael (with Tony Schwartz), Work in Progress (Penguin, 1998); Ford, Henry, My Life and Work (Doubleday, 1923); Gerstner, Louis, Who Says Elephants Can't Dance? (HarperBusiness, 2002); Guinness, Jonathan, Requiem for a Family Business (Macmillan, 1997); Iacocca, Lee (with William Novak), Iacocca (Bantam, 1984); Iverson, Ken, Plain Talk (Wiley & Sons, 1998); Rathenau, Walter, In Days to Come (Allen &

Unwin, 1921); Rockefeller, John D., *Random Reminiscences of Men and Events* (1909); Sculley, John (with John Byrne), *Odyssey: From Pepsico to Apple*...(HarperCollins, 1987); Selfridge, H. Gordon, *The Romance of Commerce* (J. Lane, 1918); Sloan, Alfred (with John McDonald), *My Years with General Motors* (Doubleday, 1963); Walton, Sam (with John Huey), *Made in America* (Doubleday, 1992); Watson, Thomas Jnr, *Father, Son & Co* (Bantam, 1990); Welch, Jack (with John Byrne), *Straight From The Gut* (Warner, 2001). Alphabetically by subject, the following biographies were consulted: Hagstrom, Robert, *The Warren Buffett Way* (Allen & Unwin, 1994); Byrne, John, *Chainsaw: The Notorious Career of Al Dunlap in the Era of Profit-at-any-Price* (HarperBusiness, 1999); Lacey, Robert, *Ford: The Men and the Machine* (Heinemann, 1986); Wright, J. Patrick, *On A Clear Day You Can See General Motors: John Z. De Lorean's Look Inside the Automotive Giant* (Wright Enterprises, 1979); Wyden, Peter, *The Unknown Iacocca* (William Morrow, 1987); Blainey, Geoffrey, *The Steelmaster* (Melbourne University Press, 1971); Chernow, Ron, *Titan: A Life of John D. Rockefeller Snr* (Warner, 1998); Hessen, Robert, *Steel Titan: The Life of Charles M. Schwab* (Oxford University Press, 1975); Farber, David, *Sloan Rules* (University of Pennsylvania Press, 2002).

Investment and Economics

The classic work on investment cycles is Charles Mackay's *Extraordinary Popular Delusions and the Madness of Crowds* (Richard Bentley, 1841). I have also quoted: Galbraith, John Kenneth, *The Great Crash of 1929* (Houghton Mifflin, 1997); Haas, Albert and Don Jackson, *Bulls, Bears and Dr Freud: Why You Win Or Lose on the Stock Market* (World Publishing, 1965); Shiller, Robert, *Irrational Exuberance* (Princeton University Press, 2000). The last outbreak of 'irrational exuberance' is well documented from the outside by John Cassidy's *dot.con: The Greatest Story Ever Sold* (Penguin, 2002), and from the inside in Ernst Malmsten's *boo hoo: $135 million, 18 months...A dot.com story from concept to catastrophe* (Business Books, 2001) and James J. Cramer's *Confessions of a Street Addict* (Simon & Schuster, 2002). Information on Enron is drawn from: Fusaro, Peter C. and Ross M. Miller, *What Went Wrong at Enron* (Wiley, 2002); McLean, Bethany and Peter Elkind, *The Smartest Guys in the Room* (Penguin, 2003); Swartz, Mimi (with Sherron Watkins), *Power Failure: The Rise and Fall of Enron* (Aurum, 2003); and two articles in the *New Yorker*, Malcolm Gladwell's 'The Talent Myth' (27 July 2002) and Jeffrey Toobin's 'End Run at Enron' (27 October 2003).

Views on agency theory and the economic consequences of corporate structures are derived from: Berle, Adolph and Gardiner Means, *The Modern Corporation and Private Property* (Macmillan, 1932); Fukuyama, Francis, Trust: The Social Virtues and the Creation of Prosperity (Free Press, 1995); Olson, Mancur, The Logic of Collective Actions: Public Goods and the Theory of Groups (Harvard University Press, 1965); Wiles, P. J. D., Price, Cost and Output (Blackwell, 1958); Williamson, Oliver, The Nature of the Firm: Origins, Evolution and Development (Oxford University Press, 1993). Two provocative works on rewards and their entailments are Derek Bok's The Cost of Talent (Free Press, 1993) and Alfie Kohn's Punished By Rewards (Houghton Mifflin, 1995). Mathew Hayward and Donald Hambrick proposed a connection between acquisition and ego in 'Explaining the Premiums Paid for Large Acquisitions: Evidence of CEO Hubris', a contribution to Administrative Quarterly (no. 42, 1997). The relationship between executive ownership and corporate performance is studied by Dan Dalton, Catherine Daily and Nandini Rajagopalan in 'Governance Through Ownership' in the American Management Journal (April 2003). Findings on Australian mergers by Tim Brailsford and Stephen Knights are from 'Mergers and Takeovers: Should We Be Concerned?' in How Big Business Performs (Allen & Unwin, 1999). 'Tournament theory' was outlined by Sherwin Rosen and Jeffrey Lazear in 'Rank Order Tournaments as Optimum Labor Contracts' in the Journal of Political Economy (October 1981). Paul Samuelson's quote is from Robert Heilbroner's The Worldly Philosophers (Penguin, 2000).

Other Journal Articles
This essay draws heavily on reportage from The Economist, Fortune, Forbes, Fast Company, Business 2.0, CFO, Eurobusiness, Worth, Businessweek, Business Review Weekly, Time and Newsweek. Booz Allen Hamilton's splendid survey 'CEO Succession 2002: Deliver or Depart' was published in strategy + business (Summer 2003). Two excellent collections were extremely useful: Best Business Crime Writing of the Year (Anchor, 2002), edited by James Surowiecki, and The New Gilded Age: New Yorker Looks at the New Culture of Affluence (Modern Library, 2001), edited by David Remnick. Notwithstanding its quaint solicitation of subscriptions, Harvard Business Review from time to time lives up to its reputation as business's most influential magazine. Contributions cited or quoted by this essay are, in chronological order: 'Selecting Strategies That Create Shareholder Value' (May–June 1981) by Alfred Rappaport; 'The Coming of the New Organisation' (January–February 1988) by Peter Drucker; 'The Eclipse of the Public Corporation' (September–October 1989) and 'It's Not How Much You Pay, But How' (May–June 1990) by Michael Jensen; 'The Logic of Global Business: An Interview with ABB's Percy Barnevik' (March–April 1991) by William Taylor; 'The Promise of the Governed Corporation' by John Pound

(March–April 1995); 'Bringing Silicon Valley Inside' by Gary Hamel (September–October 1999); 'Don't Hire The Wrong CEO' by Warren Bennis and James O'Toole (May-June 2000);'What Makes Great Boards Great' by Jeffrey Sonnenfeld (September–October 2002); 'Holes at the Top: Why CEO Firings Backfire' by Margarethe Wiersema (November–December 2002). Keith Jackson is quoted from 'Ten Money Notes' in *Granta* 49 (Winter 1994). Jeff Madrick is quoted from 'Welch's Juice' in the *New York Review of Books* (12 February 2002).

Miscellaneous

The following works of fiction are quoted from or referred to: Christie, Agatha, *The Seven Dials Mystery* (Collins, 1929); Dickens, Charles, *Dombey & Son* (Bradbury & Evans, 1853); Dreiser, Theodore, *The Financier* (Harper & Brothers, 1912); Galsworthy, John, *The Skin Game* (Duckworth, 1920); Heller, Joseph, *Something Happened* (Corgi, 1974); Hemingway, Ernest, *The Sun Also Rises* (Scribner, 1926); Levin, Ira, *The Stepford Wives* (Book Club, 1972); Lardner, Ring, *A Ring Lardner Reader* (Viking, 1946); Lodge, David, *Nice Work* (Secker & Warburg, 1988); Mann, Thomas, *Buddenbrooks* (Everyman's Library, 1994); Marquand, J. P., *Sincerely, Willis Wayde* (Little, Brown, 1954); O'Neill, Eugene, *A Moon for the Misbegotten* (Random House, 1952); Rand, Ayn, *Atlas Shrugged* (Random House, 1957); Trollope, Anthony, *The Way We Live Now* (Chapman & Hall, 1875); Wells, H. G., *The World of William Clissold* (John Murray, 1926). Films cited are: *Executive Suite* (director: Robert Wise, 1954); *The Man In the Gray Flannel Suit* (director: Nunnally Johnson, 1956); *Other People's Money* (director: Norman Jewison, 1991); *Patterns* (director: Fielder Cook, 1956); *Silent Movie* (director: Mel Brooks, 1976); *Wall Street* (director: Oliver Stone, 1987). George Santayana is quoted from *The Life of Reason* (John Murray, 1905), Isaiah Berlin from *Conversations with Henry Brandon* (Deutsch, 1966), Hans Keller from *Criticism* (Faber & Faber, 1987).